SUMMER OF '78

SUMMER OF '78

A Road Trip

BY GREG HARRIS

ISBN: 9781098743765

In memory of
David Warren Fralia
God rest his soul.
January 24, 1960–May 4, 1993

WASHINGTON

PORTLAND

OREGON

MONTANA

WEST
YELLOW-
STONE

BOISE

IDAHO
FALLS

JACKSON

IDAHO

WYOMING

SACRAMENTO

NEVADA

SALT
LAKE
CITY

SAN JOSE

CALIFORNIA

UTAH

LAS
VEGAS

ARIZONA

LOS ANGELES

SAN DIEGO

MEXICO

SUMMER OF '78

TOTAL MILES - 3,340
- - - INTERSTATE
. . . . U.S. / STATE HIGHWAY

N

A GRAND ADVENTURE

"**G**oddammit, Fralia, focus! Where's your head at?" yells the coach.

I'm thinking to myself, *Oh, boy. Here we go again.*

It's senior year in high school and none of us are focusing, but Fralia is always an easy target. And why not—he's good looking, charismatic, and smooth talking, and he's dating the hottest girl in school. It seems like even the coaches are jealous of his charmed life.

Dave Fralia was the first person I met when I moved to San Diego. It was at "two-a-days" practice for frosh football at Mount Carmel before the school year began. We just hit it off and became fast friends.

That was 1974, and now here we are in May of 1978, and graduation can't come soon enough. The day after graduation, we are jumping in Herman, my 1970 Volkswagen Bug, and hitting the road for a five-week trip of the Western United States. A grand adventure: a two-man tent, our fishing poles, and .22 caliber rifles in the back seat. Everyone thinks we are just talking shit. Oh, ye of little faith. I'm only seventeen, but I will be eighteen in a week and a half after graduation.

We have a nice loop planned through Nevada, Utah, Idaho, Wyoming, Montana, down the Oregon coastline, and back into California. We'll be visiting my friend in Idaho Falls. I lived there for three years, the formative ones, between eleven and thirteen. Idaho was fun, but San Diego is more to my liking. Toward the end of the trip, we'll be in Sacramento, my birthplace, visiting my aunt, cousins, and childhood friends. Our last stop will be San Jose to visit our friend, Suzie.

You are probably thinking, *Herman? Who names their car that? Isn't a guy's car supposed to be a she?* Well, Herman *is* a she. The Encinitas Herman Cook license plate frame inspired the name. I got a great deal at $650. She's a faded red without dings or dents. She always starts, is dependable, and—like most Bugs—leaks a little oil. The gas gauge also doesn't work, but the trip odometer does, so I just have to be sure to get gas around 240 miles. I've only run out of gas a few times, but I always carry a skateboard and a gas can in the front hood for when it happens. Herman has a roof rack, and we plan on taking the bench seat out of the rear and folding the back down for more storage room. She has a new set of bias ply tires. She's good to go.

A critical component of any road trip is music—I just got a swinging deal at Pacific Stereo on a Pioneer AM/FM cassette deck. None of our tapes are going to get eaten! We are each bringing a briefcase full of tapes. Killer mix tapes and plenty of Neil, REO, Steve Miller, Elton John, Ted, Frampton, Stones, America, Lynyrd Skynyrd, Rush, April Wine, and even some Jimmy Buffett, just to name a few.

But graduation is still weeks away, and the days just drag on. We are in no-man's-land: senioritis, completely done with high school, but still stuck in it. We spend our days putting forth minimal effort and screwing around: blowing off classes, running an underground newspaper, hitting the beach, and dreaming about our grand adventure.

DAY ONE

Fralia, Jules, myself, and MK

We are so excited to leave that neither of us sleep. I pick Fralia up before sunrise; he hangs his graduation tassel over the rearview mirror and says, "Now we're ready to go!"

A few miles later:

"Dude, quit shaking your leg. You're driving me nuts with the constant tapping on the floorboard," I say.

"Goddamn!" Fralia says. "Just get me out of Escondido."

There is no one on the road, yet we're stopping at every light.

"Did you hear they're going to build a freeway just west of us that will bypass Escondido?" I ask.

Fralia, with a real unexplained hatred for Escondido, says, "Good! That will be the best thing to ever happen to this shit-hole city."

I have to agree. Escondido is an anticlimactic start to our grand adventure. It takes us over an hour, but we are finally out of San Diego County.

The sun rises as we drive through Rancho California.

In 1978, it was unfathomable to think that Temecula would grow as much as it has.

"There's a lot of nothing out here," I comment.

"It's better than Escondido," Fralia responds. "Are you ready for some music? How about a little Steve Miller, *Fly Like an Eagle?*"

"Sure, Fralia. Stick it in. Did you bring the Foghat tape?"

"I've told you a million times—I don't have a Foghat tape. That was my sister's, and it's an eight-track!"

"What?" I say. "Connie still has an eight-track player?"

"Yes! How many times do I have to explain this to you? She's old—twenty-two—and has a big collection of eight-tracks. So she's just going to keep playing them until the player craps out. Geez, we've been with her like two times in her car, and you can't stop talking about Foghat!"

"Well, I also remember her playing Crosby, Stills, Nash and Young's 'Love the One You're With,' and her going on and on about how that's her new motto to live by," I say, grinning.

"You're lucky you don't have sisters. It's one drama after another with her."

"Your sister is cool," I say.

"Huh, you'd think differently if she was your sister," he says.

"Do you think you can make it to Barstow before needing to piss?" I ask. "That's a good spot for us to gas up."

"Yeah, I can make Barstow. You just keep driving. And don't worry. I've got the music all lined up. After Steve Miller, we'll do *2112*. Then *Double Live Gonzo!*"

"Dude. Is your chick, Julie, really from Barstow?" I ask. "Yes."

"It's just hard for me to imagine a chick as hot as her being from Barstow. Maybe Barstow is like an unknown secret breeding ground for smoking-hot chicks."

"Geez, Harris, sometimes I can't believe the things that come out of your mouth—'unknown secret breeding ground'? What the fuck? Barstow is nothing but a shithole, maybe even a bigger shithole than Escondido. And there's no way any chick still stuck in that town is hotter than Jules."

"Maybe when we get gas, we'll drive around Barstow just to verify there are no hot chicks," I say.

"Take my word for it—there are no hot chicks. We are pissing and gassing up. Then we're heading north."

He is right. We don't see anything close to a hot chick in Barstow.

"Where are the maps?" he asks.

"Geez. Where do you think they are? Duh, look in the glove box," I tell him.

"How far should we try to get today?" Fralia inquires.

"Salt Lake for sure. Maybe beyond," I say. "The further we get today, the shorter tomorrow's drive will be to Idaho Falls."

"Sounds good."

After looking at the map, Fralia says, "Littlefield? Beaver Dam, Arizona? I didn't realize we went through Arizona! Sounds like a good place for our second stop—get some ice and snacks."

"Sure, that's probably about right on mileage: Barstow to Beaver Dam," I say. "The last thing we want is to run out of gas in the middle of the hot desert. Do you think you can figure out the mileage?"

"Fuck! Of course, I can. Just hold on…it's looking like two hundred and fifty miles."

"Could be close—two hundred and forty miles is when I like to get gas. Since it's all freeway, maybe we can pull it off."

Fralia says, "Let's roll the dice."

Although it's only ten in the morning as we drive through Baker, you can see the heat radiating off the asphalt.

"Hot weather means Jimmy Buffett. And I'm not feeling this Ted Nugent shit," I say.

"You and your Jimmy Buffett. Just let me hear 'Stranglehold,' and I'll put Jimmy in for you."

"Put in *Changes in Latitudes*."

"Duh."

"That should get us to State Line, " I say.

Sure as shit, "Landfall," the last song on the tape, starts playing, and I see State Line, Nevada.

"Say goodbye to the Golden State."

"Goodbye, Golden State. Hello, Silver State," says Fralia.

At high noon on a hot summer day, Vegas doesn't look very glamorous. Instead, it's kind of stark and ugly. Dollars to doughnuts, I knew Fralia would want to stop in Vegas. I hate Vegas.

"Harris, we have to stop in Vegas! How could we not? Let's try to get into a casino!"

"What the fuck for?"

"Roulette table! I'm feeling lucky," he says. "And maybe get a shrimp cocktail or a hotdog."

"Dude! You're eighteen. I'm seventeen. We aren't getting into any goddamn casino. So forget it! Let's keep driving."

"Oh, come on, pussy," he badgers me.

"Just to tease you, we'll drive down the strip, but we aren't stopping."

"What a dick."

"You'll get over it," I say. "Next stop: Arizona."

As we drive on, I keep staring at the trip odometer and speedometer. Trying to hold steady at fifty-five miles per hour, praying we don't run out of gas.

"Okay, twenty miles to Beaver Dam, according to the trip odometer," I state.

"Damn, it's hot out. It's gotta be over one hundred degrees. Thank *God* for the wing vents," Fralia says.

"No shit! Can you imagine if we didn't have them?"

"Yeah, we'd be dead."

"Beaver Dam better have a store, and they better have Gatorade. A Hostess chocolate pie would also be good," I say.

"And a couple of Abba-Zaba bars!"

"You brought three hundred in cash, right?" I ask, wanting to verify.

"Yup. So did you, right?"

"Yes," I say.

Everything we want, the Beaver Dam store has. We drive down the street to a shaded park, put ice in the cooler, have our snacks, and take off. I quickly get behind a semi and draft off him. The guy is sucking us along, eighty miles per hour, and I'm not even on the gas. We are just getting ready to enter the Virgin River Gorge when out of nowhere, John Law is on our tail. He hits his lights and siren, so we pull over.

"Fuck, fuck, FUCK!" I yell. "I can't believe I'm getting a ticket. Fuck."

"Ha, ha! You fucked up, Harris. This cop is going to nail you."

"Hello, officer," I calmly say as he walks up to the car.

"Hello, boys. Do you know why I stopped you?"

"Speeding?" I ask.

"You were definitely speeding, and you also appear to be stupid. Drafting off of semis is not a good idea. They can't see you in their mirrors when you're that close. It's a good way to get killed. Do you understand me, son?"

"Yes, sir," I say.

"I'm actually pulling you over for littering."

We are both completely puzzled. "Littering?"

"Yes, littering. Your passenger left an empty ice bag with Abba-Zaba wrappers in the park back in Beaver Dam."

Fralia speaks up. "Sir, I assure you that was an honest mistake. We are not litterbugs. It must've accidentally fallen out. Our parents didn't raise us to be litterbugs."

"Honest mistake or not, son, I'm writing you a ticket for littering."

"So," I ask, "no ticket for me?"

"Warning for you, for speeding and drafting. Ticket for your pal, the litterbug."

I'm grinning ear to ear, doing my best to keep from laughing. It's funny how some adults can completely see through Fralia's shit.

"Where are you California boys going?"

"Idaho Falls," I answer.

"Why?" he asks.

"I used to live there. We're visiting some friends."

The cop says to Fralia, "License, please, Mister Smooth Talker."

"How much is this going to cost me?" Fralia asks.

"You'll have to call this number and speak to Judge Heaton. Have a good day, boys. Now get out of Arizona."

The cop isn't even back to his cruiser, and I am laughing my ass off.

"Mister Smooth Talker! Ha, good one! I can't wait to tell everyone this story. He saw right through your shitty Eddie Haskell imitation. You're such a dumb fuck."

"Fuck you and Arizona!" Fralia fumes. "Get me out of this state!"

I obediently follow the speed limit through the Virgin River Gorge and get out of Arizona and into Utah.

"Let's switch drivers in Saint George," he says.

"Okay, Fralia, but only if you promise not to litter!"

"Is this how it's going to be?"

"Yup," I say, laughing.

"I can't believe he didn't ticket your ass. What a lucky fuck."

"Better to be a lucky fuck than a dumb fuck. How did you manage to leave the bag?" I ask.

"I swear I thought I put it in the back seat. That bastard must've been watching us. I don't think it will affect my insurance rates, but it's going to cost me for sure. When we get to your friend's house tomorrow, I'm going to call that judge. Take the first exit we come to in Saint George," he says.

"Okay, and if you're wondering what a Mormon looks like, this is your golden opportunity. They're the only people who live in Saint George," I tell him.

The first exit has a gas station, so we decide we might as well top off the tank while switching drivers.

"Okay, it's your turn to drive. Take us all the way to Salt Lake City. Well, what do you think of the few Mormons you just saw?" I say.

"White as white can be."

"Ha, you think?" I say.

"I do."

"Well, they're very polite to your face, but they're definitely clannish and cult-like, like most religious people."

"To each his own, I guess," he says.

"Let's grab some dinner in Salt Lake, and after that, we'll start thinking about where we'll spend the night," I tell him.

"Sounds great. Pop in some good music," he says.

I pop in *REO Speedwagon Live*, recline my seat, relax, and adjust the wing vent so the warm air is blasting my face. Grinning ear to ear and listening to "(Only a) Summer Love," I think about how great it is to be out of high school and on the road. Gary's guitar sounds so good that I rewind it and play the song again full blast with my eyes closed. Damn, I'm happy.

The next song is "Son of a Poor Man," and we both start banging on the dashboard like it's a piano. We are ecstatic.

"Look, Fralia, seventy-two miles to Beaver. Do you want to stop there?"

"Hell, no. After the Beaver Dam, Arizona, debacle, I'm definitely not stopping in Beaver, Utah, or any other town with Beaver in it."

"Okay, keep driving. After Salt Lake, I'll drive again. I could really go for a shower after sweating my balls off all day. Let's shoot for Lava Hot Springs, Idaho. There's a KOA there. They have showers and a swimming pool. Then that'll give us less than a two-hour drive to Idaho Falls tomorrow," I say.

We tank up in Salt Lake City, switch drivers, and have a quick bite to eat at Burger Chef.

"Welcome to Idaho, Fralia! Look at us—our fifth state today. If I remember correctly, it should be about an hour to Lava Hot Springs."

"I love it!" he says. "Five states. What a day."

Fifteen hours after leaving San Diego, we roll into Lava Hot Springs with just enough light to set up camp. Still high on adrenaline from graduation and hitting the road, neither of us is tired. We call our moms—collect—to tell them where we are. And of course, I tell my mom about Fralia's littering ticket.

IDAHO FALLS

"**D**ude, you really lived in this state?" asks Fralia.

"Sure did. Three long years surrounded by Mormons."

"Is your buddy a Mormon?"

"No, Robert's trouble," I tell him.

"What do you mean?"

"You'll see in a few hours when you meet him."

"Oh, come on. Tell me some stories."

"I shouldn't have said he was trouble. Now I've already tainted your view of him. And besides, maybe he's changed. That was all a long time ago."

"Come on, one story," pleads Fralia.

"Okay. In the eighth grade, when we weren't that close, he cold-cocked the school bus driver. When he was exiting the bus, he just turned and slugged him in the face. It literally knocked the old guy out and broke his jaw."

"Why did he do it?"

"Dude, I have no idea."

My friendship with Robert was based on us knowing each other in Sacramento. We were in the same second grade class at Sequoia Elementary. He moved to Idaho Falls after second grade. When you are that young, you easily lose track of friends who move.

We moved to Idaho Falls toward the end of my fifth-grade year. I remember the first day like it was yesterday.

"Good morning, class," said my new teacher, Mrs. Drew. "We have a new student this morning. Please welcome Greg Harris. He just moved here from Sacramento, California."

From the back of the class, everyone heard Robert: "Hey! I know you! Greg, it's Robert! We were in the same class in second grade in Sacramento. You used to come over to my house after school."

"Hey," I responded, smiling and feeling totally relieved. I knew someone; it wouldn't be that bad.

Mrs. Drew said, "Well, isn't this a nice coincidence. Greg, please take a seat by Robert. Robert, please introduce Greg to everyone at recess and show him around."

Once we moved to San Diego, my mom often said, "Gregory, thank God I got you out of Idaho Falls. You'd be in jail or, worse, dead if we had stayed. Robert James can't help it, but he has a mean streak."

She was right. Robert was fairly normal in second and fifth grade, but in the sixth grade, he started to become erratic... and began lifting weights. Being in the white state of Idaho, he had no interactions with other races. He started saying negative and outright mean things about blacks, Mexicans, and Asians. I believe he got it from his mom.

While in the seventh grade, Robert and I had a few brushes with the law—mostly vandalism stuff and one breaking and entering, which we thought was bogus.

Robert and I were into raising pigeons. We both had coops in our backyards. One day, while riding our bikes past the old boarded-up junior high school, we saw a bunch of pigeons flying in and out of the second-story broken windows. What caught our eyes were the pigeons that were doing backflips in midflight—Tumbler pigeons! We'd only read about Tumbler pigeons. Neither of us had ever seen them. We didn't even know they could be found in Idaho. We were amazed at their acrobatics and wanted some as pets.

So we devised a plan to break in at night while the pigeons were roosting. Armed with flashlights and burlap potato sacks, we were going to catch as many as we could—hoping some would be Tumblers.

The building was silent when we pried open the piece of plywood covering the front entrance. While walking up the stairs, we heard the pigeons beginning to coo and move around. We stopped, both of us with an index finger at our lips. We waited for a few minutes for them to calm back down so we could catch them by surprise. Whispering, I told Robert, "On the count of three, let's charge in." He was to run toward the broken windows, I was to shoo them his direction, and he would catch as many as he could.

I whispered, "One, two, three, go!"

We bolted in and, immediately, Robert slipped and fell because the floor was covered in pigeon shit. And then so was he!

I yelled, "Get up! Go to the windows! They're all escaping!"

It was absolute bedlam and pitch dark except for the dim rays of light from our cheap flashlights. There were far more pigeons than we'd imagined—they flew all over the place, bounced off our bodies, and hit our heads. We threw up our arms, tried to protect our faces, and screamed, "Fuck! Shit!" and every other expletive we knew as twelve-year-olds. The smart ones escaped, and we caught two sacks of dumb ones.

The plan was to go back to his garage, pull them out of the sacks one at a time, keep the Tumblers, and release the regular pigeons.

Unfortunately, as we exited the school, there were the cops—waiting for us. While driving by, they saw the flashlights through the broken windows. For the life of them, they couldn't believe we were upstairs catching pigeons. But there we were with potato sacks full of them and one of us covered in pigeon shit. They laughed, then made us release all the birds. They hauled us into the cop station and threatened us with breaking-and-entering charges. Needless to say, they called our parents. Robert's dad was out of town, so it was only his mom and both of my parents. After what seemed like an eternity, the three parents convinced the cops that they would severely punish us.

By eighth grade, my parents got smart and insisted I stay away from Robert, so we kind of drifted apart. Then we moved to San Diego.

◆ ◆ ◆

Driving through Blackfoot, I say, "There's the Snake River."

"No shit? Wow! Where did Evel Knievel try jumping it?"

"That was down by Twin Falls. We aren't going that way."

"Evel is a badass," Fralia admiringly says.

We roll into Idaho Falls around noon. I show him the falls. He isn't impressed. We drive by the house I lived in on Sahara Drive, then go a couple more blocks to Robert's house. When we pull up, he's in the driveway with his shirt off, waxing his green '69 Firebird. I shouldn't have been surprised, but, damn, Robert is muscle-bound. Fralia has one word to say: "Steroids."

"Hey, Harris," says Robert in his Idaho dialect.

"Robert, geez! Look at you. Holy shit! You're a big bastard. This is my friend, Dave Fralia."

"Nice to meet you," they both say and shake hands. That was probably the last time they shook hands.

"Rick is on his way over," Robert says. "I figure we'll have lunch. You guys hungry?"

"Are we ever!" I respond. "Rick is a year older than us, right?"

"Yes. I'm sure you'll remember him. Big blond guy."

When Robert says, "Big blond guy," it jogs my memory. Nice enough guy, but he should've added the adjective "dumb" to his description. He finishes waxing his car, and we eat peanut butter sandwiches, Frito chips, and milk. Robert is a big milk guy.

"So what should we do today?" I ask.

"Once Rick gets here, let's go to the sand dunes. Sometimes there are girls sunbathing topless," Robert says, all excited, in what seems like a high-pitched voice.

Fralia is quieter than usual.

"What? Since when do chicks go topless in Idaho Falls?" is my astonished reply.

"There are a handful of girls who aren't Mormon and wish they lived in California."

Fralia asks Robert if he can use the phone for a long-distance call to Arizona. Robert responds that his mom won't care.

Fralia gets on the phone. "Hello, may I speak to Judge Heaton?"

A moment later: "Good afternoon, Your Honor. My name is David...David Warren Fralia. I was issued a littering ticket yesterday."

Another moment passes: "Yes, sir. I understand, sir. I'd like to plead guilty...with an explanation."

After a slight pause, Fralia says, "Yes, sir. I understand. Thank you," and hangs up the phone.

Dying to know, I say, "Soooo?"

"Motherfucker!" he says. "A hundred goddamn dollars! I hate that state!"

Another thing about Robert is that he fancies himself an impersonator, and he is actually quite good at it.

"'Good afternoon, Your Honor. My name is David...David Warren Fralia. I'd like to plead guilty...with an explanation,'" parrots Robert, nailing Fralia's voice to a tee.

Robert and I laugh. Fralia doesn't. So, naturally, Robert does it again.

"'Good afternoon, Your Honor. My name is David...David Warren Fralia. I'd like to plead guilty...with an explanation.'"

And again and again.

Fralia finds no humor in it. Throughout the rest of the day, Robert, out of nowhere, busts out his impersonation. "'My name is David...David Warren Fralia. I'd like to plead guilty...with an explanation.'" No wonder Robert and Fralia never liked each other.

Robert's friend, Rick, finally shows up, and Fralia meets him. We tell Robert we want to put some stuff in our room. He says, "Cool. Rick and I will be in the garage."

When we get into our room, Fralia says, "Is it me, or is Rick a big, dumb white guy?"

"That didn't take you long to figure out," I say.

"What in the fuck have you gotten us into?"

"Don't worry. We're sleeping in a bed tonight and leaving tomorrow. Then just seeing them again on my birthday. And probably never again after that."

The sand dunes are a complete bust. Not only are there no topless chicks—there are no chicks, period. Rick said that only once had they seen a topless girl at the sand dunes and that her breasts were nothing more than mosquito bites. But ever since that one time, Robert keeps going back, hoping for more topless girls.

"Hey, Robert. Let's go up to Taylor Mountain since we're already halfway there." Ribbing the guy, I say, "Maybe there will be some topless chicks."

"Ha, ha," says Robert.

Fralia laughs, then Rick follows.

"Okay, you dicks. Jump in my car, and we'll go up there to see nothing."

"Are the chairlifts still there?" I ask.

"Yes. It's changed quite a bit since we used to ride our bikes up there. We can't run the lifts anymore, and all the windows at the lodge are broken. But we can still climb on the chairlifts and screw around."

"So they don't ski there anymore?" Fralia wants to know.

Robert responds, "No. As long as I've been here, it has never operated."

We get up there, and Fralia says, "This is it?"

"This is it," the three of us say in unison.

I can sense Fralia is about to say something dickish, but he holds his tongue.

After an hour of shooting the shit and screwing around, Robert says, "Damn. I didn't leave my mom a note. We better get home. My dad is out of town on business, and my mom will be worrying that I'm in trouble again."

While driving back, Fralia says to Rick, "You don't talk much, do you?"

Rick responds, "Nope."

When we get back to Robert's house, his mom, Madge, is puffing Virginia Slims and pacing on the front porch.

Robert gets in front of the situation and apologizes for not leaving a note. He hugs her and then introduces Fralia.

Madge asks me, "How's your mom doing?"

"Great. Still bowling," is my only reply.

"Do you like living with all the Mexicans at the border?" she says.

I say, "I do," knowing it would give her a rise. She just looks at me and shakes her head.

Madge invites Rick to stay for dinner with the rest of us. "Sloppy Joes, tater tots, and salad."

Madge is the only mom I know who smokes during dinner. After dinner, she says, "Robert, I'd prefer if you guys just stay in tonight."

"Mom. Come on."

"No. You know you can't afford to get into any more trouble, and I remember how you and Greg behaved together."

"It's cool, Robert," I say. "We can just stay in. We brought our yearbooks. You're not going to believe all the hot chicks at our high school."

Robert says, "I have no doubt they're hotter than all the Mormon girls around here!"

Rick just chuckles and shakes his head.

We show them all the pictures of our girlfriends and ourselves.

"I can't believe all the blondes," says Robert. "Are the beaches really full of girls in bikinis?"

"Not only are they *full*—there are some spots where girls go topless," Fralia says.

"Shut up! Really?"

"Yes," I say.

"Tell me which blonde you like the best," Fralia tells Robert.

Robert leafs through the pages, stops, and puts his finger on Shelly. "That one."

Fralia, playing the big man, says, "I'm good friends with her. I'll tell you what. You come to San Diego to visit, and I'll guarantee you a date with her."

"Shut up! Really?" Robert says again.

"Really," says Fralia.

"Harris, is he lying to me?"

"If he says it, you can believe it," I say.

"Then I'm coming to San Diego."

"Well, you just dream about her. Fralia and I are ready to hit the hay and blast out of here early tomorrow. Where should we meet on my birthday?"

Robert says, "How about the town square in West Yellowstone at three?"

"Sounds great," I say.

"Don't tell my mom about it."

"We won't. But you'll be there for sure, right?" I ask.

"Yes. Rick and I will be there."

We wake up early and hightail it out of Idaho Falls.

"Harris, that town is a bigger shithole than Escondido. Taylor Mountain is what they do for fun? Good God. Get us out of here. By the way, your friend is mental. And what's with his mom and that Mexican comment?"

"Well, it's certainly not San Diego. And you're right: I'm concerned about Robert. He definitely has a screw loose. As far as his mom goes, I don't know what to say."

"Let's ditch the guy and not show up to meet him on your birthday."

"I can't do that—have the guy drive a hundred miles and us not even be there," I say. "That wouldn't be right. And why did you even entice him to come to San Diego with the promise of Shelly?"

"Christ, I don't know. You know how I get—acting all cool."

"Well, trust me, that was a mistake you'll regret."

JACKSON HOLE

Once we get out of Idaho Falls, past Rigby and Rexburg, we take the forty-mile dirt road that leads to Jackson Hole. There are many camping spots along the way. I know the area well from when I lived there. Our family used to come there often in our camper.

It has been a couple of long days filled with a lot of driving. The adrenaline is wearing off, and being out here in the Idaho wilderness, it hits home that we are actually doing it: the grand adventure.

We decide to set up camp and stay put for a few days. We fish the stream for dinner, shoot our .22s for fun, hunt rabbit one evening, and hike around the area, exploring. Rabbit is actually pretty tasty, especially the backstrap. Fralia also shoots a squirrel.

Fralia and the dead squirrel

I tell him, "If you kill it, you eat it. That's the way I was raised."

So he skins it and does the best he can to gut it. We put it on a stick and roast it over the fire. Rabbit is definitely better tasting than squirrel.

We talk about our girlfriends...and Robert James. There is a brief discussion about our futures—brief because neither of us have any idea what we want to do beyond enrolling at Palomar College, a.k.a. Poway High School with ashtrays.

The conversation naturally leads us to our next stop: Jackson Hole, Wyoming. And that gets Fralia anxious to break camp. After three days of just me, he's ready to see other people. Fralia thrives off of being around people. So he's all about a busy little tourist town.

The drinking age in Wyoming is nineteen. Fralia is convinced he'll have an easy time buying us some beer.

"Harris, I want to do some drinking and flirting and see what the Jackson Hole hype is all about."

So it's settled—we break camp.

When we roll into town, he lights up. "Harris. This is going to be great! Let's get supplies, ice, and beer, and then we can set up camp and mingle. The closer to town, the better, at least for a few days."

Sure enough, he was able to buy beer, no questions asked. This fact makes Fralia even more confident that we are going to have a great time in Jackson Hole.

The closest place for us to pitch our tent is the KOA just outside of town. I am hesitant because of the cost, but Fralia convinces me the odds are this will be our biggest camping expenditure. Most of the other stops will be free or dirt cheap.

The KOA manager tells us he likes to put the tenters up on the bluff. We know the guy is just being a dick and wants us away from all the family campers. But we don't care; this stop is about the town, not the campground.

We set up camp away from everyone else on the bluff, where we have an incredible view of the National Elk Refuge in the valley below. Sitting on our picnic table, drinking a Coors, we can barely stand how cool we are.

National Elk Refuge and Sleeping Indian Mountain

Forty years later, looking back on this time, it's amazing how full of ourselves we were. In our minds, there was no one smarter or cooler—we were young and invincible—and for a brief window of time, it really seemed like we could do no wrong. It was a self-fulfilling prophecy. Everything we thought we could do, we did. It's no wonder we thought so highly of ourselves. The reality of life hadn't caught up with us yet.

"Okay, Harris. Let's go mingle."

"Should we pack the cooler?"

"I swear to God, sometimes I worry about you," declares Fralia.

"So that's a *yes?*"

"That's a *fuck yes!*" he answers.

I cram two six-packs into the cooler, and we drive the short ten miles to town. We park on a little side road, have another beer, and then hit the streets. Fralia is really feeling it, so we buy some of our favorite cheap cigars, Rum Soaked Crooks, and a couple of fountain drinks that we intend to pour out so we can fill the cups with beer. We go back to the car, drink another beer, dump the sodas, and fill the cups with Coors. We walk over to the town square, sit underneath one of the elk antler arches, spark our cigars, and sip our beers. Feeling quite pleased with ourselves—less than a week removed from graduation—we are getting quite a few looks.

"Harris. Check out that one."

"She's hot."

"Hot and with her parents," he says. "I can't believe all the families. There are people here from all over the country. It's kind of crazy. After we finish our 'gars, let's pop our heads into some shops. The local girls will be working."

"No hurry," I say.

"No hurry," Fralia confirms.

We sit there and watch all the tourists. We even take pictures for some folks posing under the elk antler arches.

"Let's find a pizza place. We should get some food in our stomachs," Fralia says.

"Yeah. I'm hungry, but we can't burn through all of our money in the first week."

"For Christ's sake, Harris! Quit worrying. After your birthday, there are weeks of nothing until Sacramento. I guarantee we'll make it on money. And you know what? I bet I can buy a pitcher of beer with the pizza!"

Sure as shit, he buys a pitcher with our pepperoni pie. It isn't quite Round Table quality, but, damn, it tastes great, and the beer goes down so easy, we have another pitcher.

"Harris, always leave a nice tip. It's just the right thing to do. Now let's go check out the tourist traps."

After about five shops, we've seen enough. None of the girls working are cute, and they all sell the same shit. Besides, we need to watch our cash, or Fralia is going to blow through all of our money.

As we leave the last shop, I say, "Good God. You think people buy into the bullshit jackalope story?"

"Of course, they do. I bet they sell more of those postcards than any other."

"People are stupid," I say.

"Harris, according to P.T. Barnum, there's a sucker born every minute."

"No doubt."

"I really want to get into that Million Dollar Cowboy bar. Let's go try," says Fralia.

"Dude, it'll never happen."

This time I was correct. The doorman just laughs and tells us, "Beat it, kids."

"Fuck that cowboy, Harris. Let's go check out Snow King and then go back to our spot under the antlers for an evening smoke."

Darkness is setting in when we get back to the antlers.

"Harris, when we get rich, no more cheap, machine-rolled cigars."

"These aren't bad. I kind of like the rum flavor."

"Christ, I have a lot to teach you," he says. "You want to be smoking Cubans. Hand rolled on a Cuban woman's thigh—nice tight roll and a long burn. When we get to West

Yellowstone, listen to me, and follow my lead when we're bar hopping."

"Why is it you think you know so much?" I ask.

"Christ, what do you think I've been doing the last six months? There's so much I've learned bussing tables at The Ivanhoe in Poway."

I just shake my head.

"Fralia, I think I'm fucked up. Let's get back to the KOA."

"Probably a good idea. This is just a big family tourist scene, anyways."

"Do you remember where we parked Herman?" I ask.

"Geez, Harris. You *are* fucked up. Follow me."

"Are you sure it's this side street?"

"Positive," asserts Fralia.

"Okay, Mister Positive. Where's the Bug?" I ask.

"I swear this is where we parked it," he slurs.

"What are you saying?" I ask. "Do you think someone stole it?"

"Maybe."

"Oh, for Christ's sake, Fralia! No one stole it. We just don't know where it is."

"I'm telling you—it was here."

"I'm telling you we're *both* fucked up," I say.

We walk up and down each street until we finally find the faded red VW Bug with a luggage rack on top and California plates.

"We don't need to tell anyone about this, Harris."

"Agreed, Mister Positive. Let's flip a coin to see who's driving," I say.

"Okay. Heads I win, tails you lose."

"Fuck you, Fralia. You're driving."

"Give me the keys, pussy."

We make it back to the KOA, no problem. The moment we crawl into the two-man tent, the wind starts up. Then it really starts blowing, almost collapsing our tent.

Fralia is irate. "'We like to put the tenters up on the bluff,' my ass! That son of a bitch knew this was going to happen."

"Come on, the view is awesome up here. Do you really think it was intentional?"

"One hundred percent. That dick knew for sure it would be windy up here. Screw this place. We're leaving tomorrow. You just watch. That bastard will gladly give us our money back."

Because of all the wind, we don't really sleep. At sunrise, the wind dies down, and the view of the valley below is beautiful. I could've sat there all day, but Fralia has had enough after last night. So we fire up the griddle, have some pancakes and Tang, and break camp. I stay in the driver's seat while Fralia struts into the office to get our refund.

"I told you. That son of a bitch just snickered and gave back all of our money."

We drive into town and buy some more Coors, Tang, ice, mac and cheese, peanut butter, Wonder bread, and Saltines.

"I can't believe we lost Herman last night."

All Fralia has to say is, "Embarrassing."

"Tuesday's Gone" is playing as we leave town. That's it for Jackson Hole.

GRAND TETON AND YELLOWSTONE NATIONAL PARKS

The Grand Tetons

"**D**ude, we're too early to snag a campsite," I say. "I'm going to drive us to the Jenny Lake area. We'll do the Hidden Falls hike. Then go to Gros Ventre Campground."

"This is your country. I'm good with anything. It's all new to me."

"Do you know what Gros Ventre means?" I ask.

"I know Grand Tetons is big tits."

"Duh, everyone knows that."

"Well, Mister Two Years of High School French, why don't you tell me?" he says.

"Big belly."

"Big Belly Campground. Awesome," responds Fralia, while smiling.

As often as I've been here, I am still mesmerized by the beauty of the Tetons. You just can't help staring at them.

We pull up to Jenny Lake, and all Fralia can say is, "Wow. This isn't Lake Poway."

Summer is officially here and the weather is warm, so we are surprised to still see some snow on the trail. After a couple of miles, we hear the falls but still do not see them. We both comment how the falls are aptly named. Up a switchback and to the left, there they are—Hidden Falls, dropping one hundred feet. The sound is so deafening, we have to yell to talk to each other. The mist from the falls drenches us, but it feels great in the high-altitude sun.

Hiking back, Fralia says, "Why didn't we bring our fishing poles?"

"We can get away not having a fishing license in the remote areas but not in a national park. We'd be begging for a ticket. And you've already got a littering ticket!"

"Ha, ha."

"And no screwing around with the guns. We need to keep them hidden in the backseat while we're in the national parks," I tell him.

"Whoa! Harris! Look! Is that a bald eagle?"

"Fuck, yes, it is! Check it out."

"Wow! That's the first bald eagle I've ever seen!" Fralia exclaims.

"He's fishing. Let's watch him," I say.

"Hell, yes. I can't believe how big he is."

"Here he goes. He's dive bombing!"

Splash!

"Whoa!" we both shout.

The bald eagle lifts off out of the lake. We are close enough to see the rainbow trout hanging from one of the talons and water dripping from the eagle's feathers.

"Now, watch this," I tell Fralia. "He's going to turn the trout around so it's parallel to his body to make it easier to fly with."

"Whoa! That's the coolest thing ever!"

"Yup. Pretty amazing, isn't it?" I reply.

"Wow!"

We drive to Gros Ventre, set up camp, and talk about the itinerary. We decide on two nights there and then three nights at Yellowstone, which will bring us to my birthday in six days, when we head to West Yellowstone, Montana.

Fralia's turn to cook breakfast.

We fart around the Tetons for a couple days doing all the tourist things: Jackson Lake, Colter Bay, and the Death Canyon hike. Then we pull up stakes and move to Grant's Campground in Yellowstone, where we stay for another three days, seeing the Grand Canyon of the Yellowstone, Yellowstone Lake, Mammoth Hot Springs, and, of course, Old Faithful.

We are fascinated with the geothermal landscape. Both of us are amazed at Old Faithful. It's crazy that they know when it's going to blow.

However, we are most amazed with all the stupid people. What an incredible show they put on. Cars stopping in the middle of the road every time there is an animal sighting. Knuckleheads jumping out of their cars with cameras trying to get as close as possible to the deer, elk, bear, and bison—even raccoons. The only animals they aren't stopping for are squirrels and chipmunks.

We are not really ones to wish ill will on others, but we are kind of hoping someone will get gored or at least chased. We are likening it to a NASCAR race, with people wishing for a spectacular crash. People are stupid, and tourists are the worst. From afar, we watch this Asian guy with a camera convince his wife and two kids to walk slowly toward two bison. We thought for sure this was going to be our big show. We cross our fingers, and Fralia gets his camera ready. Unfortunately, they do not get gored or chased. The bison let us down. They just turn and walk away. The man is yelling at his wife in Japanese. She is yelling back. Obviously, we have no idea what is being said, but her kids are laughing and the man is stomping mad. It's fun watching families on vacation argue, even if you can't understand the language.

Fralia on Herman drinking a Coors, of course.

Time is slowing down for us. Now that we've spent seven days in a fifty-mile radius, just farting around, we're more relaxed and introspective. We wonder what our friends are doing. Probably just hanging out on the beach at D Street. We joke about our girlfriends cheating on us. Mostly, we are amazed that we are in Wyoming. Fralia is conjuring up stories to tell the guys back home.

"Let's make some phone calls on your birthday."

"Sure."

"I want to tell Dave House what we're doing. He'll spread the word."

"I have to call my mom. Maybe I'll try the girlfriend."

"Forget about her, Harris. When we get to West Yellowstone, I'll show you how to make a call."

"What in the fuck are you talking about? I know how to make a call."

"Just wait. You'll see."

I just shake my head. Fralia is so *Fralia*.

WEST YELLOWSTONE, MONTANA

"Happy birthday, Harris," Fralia says. "You're finally eighteen and legal."

"Eighteen. Holy shit. No more screwing around. Juvie hall is one thing, but prison is quite another."

"Like you've ever been in trouble," he says.

"Not since moving away from Idaho Falls. And the way I have it figured, four more weeks on the road with you, the odds of trouble greatly increase."

"Dude, we aren't stupid, and if we do something stupid, I can talk our way out of it."

"Right. Nice job talking your way out of it with Judge Heaton," I tell him.

"Let's have breakfast and get to West Yellowstone before your psycho friend, so I can scout the bars we're going to hop. And let's at least call House."

Less than an hour later, we are in Montana.

"Looks like we're going to hop about five times, and that'll be it. This place is so small, we can just walk to all the bars."

"Yeah, Fralia. It's a small town."

"Let's find a phone booth."

You can always count on a gas station having a pay phone. So we walk down the street to the Sinclair gas station. Sure enough, they have a phone booth.

"Okay, Harris. Watch and learn. Let's call House. First, dial zero for the operator."

"No shit. Thanks. I didn't know that."

"Hello, operator," he says. "I'd like to make a long-distance call and charge it to my home phone."

The operator is barely audible, but I can hear her ask, "Your name and home number?"

Fralia replies, "Ed Crane, 714-748-0812."

"And the number you'd like to call?"

"714-487-0074."

"No, you didn't!" I blurt out.

Fralia puts his finger to his lips, smiling and hushing me, and then hands me the receiver.

"Hello?"

"Hello, Mrs. House. It's Greg Harris."

"Oh, Greg! How are you and David doing?"

"We're in Montana and doing great!"

"Oh, honey! I'm so happy for you two, and happy birthday! Let me get David. He's going to be so excited to hear from you. Please be sure you call your mom."

"Of course," I say.

We can both hear Mrs. House telling David to pick up the phone.

"Hello?"

"House! What the fuck is going on?" I shout, and then think, *oh, shit—I hope Mrs. House didn't hear me.*

"Not much, birthday boy. Where are you guys?"

"We're in Montana—legal drinking age, eighteen!"

"Oh, shit!" House replies.

"Right?!"

"The first thing you need to know is the Crane family is paying for the phone call," I tell him.

The Crane family are local legends in Poway, known for their athletic prowess. They also rubbed everyone the wrong way without even trying. Ed was in our class. Fralia knew charging the call to them would absolutely delight House.

We hear laughter, and then House says, "God, that makes me happy."

We fill him in on our first week—our fifteen-hour first day, Judge Heaton, Robert James, Jackson Hole, Tetons, and Yellowstone—and then Fralia just can't help himself and blurts out, "We got fucked up in Jackson Hole and lost Herman."

"What?" House says.

"We found it eventually. I thought someone stole it, but Harris knew we were just fucked up."

"Nice job keeping the lid on the story, Fralia!" I say.

"I gotta get going or I'll be late to work," House says.

"Work! Ha, ha! Tell everyone we're doing fine," we both say.

"Will do," responds House.

We hang up and don't know what to do or where to go next. Finally, I say, "We still have a few hours to kill until Robert and Rick show up. Let's inventory our supplies and go to the store."

While inventorying, I notice a substantial puddle of oil under the VW.

"This isn't good," I tell Fralia.

"Shit. In Montana...with car problems," he says.

"Add oil to the shopping list. We better get three quarts," I tell him.

"What happens if the engine blows? We'll have to call your brother and have him rebuild it."

"You're so stupid. Do you think he's just going to drive out, turn a few wrenches, and solve the problem?"

"Sure, he can do it," states Fralia.

"He can do it, but it's a little more involved than that. It's not exactly a side-of-the-road job," I say.

"Unlike you, Harris, I'm an optimist. Herman won't let us down."

"Here's what we'll do," I say. "Let's cut a gallon water jug so it fits under the car. Every time we stop, we'll quickly put it underneath to catch the oil. Then when we leave, we'll pour it back into the engine. Let's just always check the oil level. And always carry a couple quarts of oil up front in the hood, just in case."

"You're not as stupid as everyone says you are."

I just shake my head and tell him to fuck off.

The grocery store is like walking back in time to the 1950s. Employees are wearing white dress shirts with ties, dark pants, aprons, and feather dusters. The store is small but well stocked and very clean.

Fralia has the list, so I'm pushing the cart. We get three cans of Quaker thirty weight oil, Tang, a couple jugs of water, and enough food to last until the next stop. Plus a twelve-pack of Coors for $3.88, which Fralia says is a great deal, and, of course, ice. Fralia also insists on two cans of Van Camp's pork and beans. I'm not a picky eater, but I'm not a fan of Van Camp's.

When we were planning this trip, we really didn't think about the expense of ice. But you need it unless you are eating shitty freeze-dried food and don't want any cold beer. We buy it, it melts, we buy more, it melts, and again and again. As often as we go into the cooler, we are lucky to go three days before needing more ice. We need to adjust our food and drink habits for the next stretch through Idaho. Originally, we envisioned seven to ten days of no civilization. I'm starting to think that's a long time with only Fralia.

"What are you thinking about, Harris?"

"Nothing. Just kind of jelling."

"Well, quit jelling. Get out your wallet. You're buying, and, hopefully, getting carded, birthday boy! And remember, it's never about getting in the shortest line; it's about getting in the cutest cashier's line. Don't forget that."

"Especially when buying condoms, right?" I say.

"Damn right, Harris. Looks like my time with you hasn't been a total waste. At least you learned that."

I just roll my eyes and shake my head. The cutest cashier wasn't that cute, and she didn't even card me.

"Let's load up and wait for your psycho friend," Fralia says.

Robert may be a psycho, but's he a dependable and on-time psycho. Right at three, we see Robert's green Firebird roll into town. He parks in front of the town square. We walk over and meet him and Rick.

"Happy birthday!" they both say.

Robert says, "Follow me. I know of a campground just a few miles north of town past the airport. We can set up camp, leave your Bug there, and all pile into my car."

So we follow Robert to this great campground, Bakers Hole, right on the Madison River. We park Herman at the first vacant site, and put the cut gallon of water container under the engine to catch the oil.

Fralia claps his hands and says, "Who's ready for a Coors?"

Of course, we all are. After everyone's first sip, Robert breaks into his impersonation. "'Good afternoon, Your Honor. My name is David...David Warren Fralia. I'd like to plead guilty...with an explanation.'"

Fralia just takes it and is smart enough to know if he says anything—anything at all—it will encourage Robert to do it more. I'm hoping a few more drinks and Fralia's promise of a date with Shelly will get us through the night without them fighting.

As we pile into the Firebird, Rick says, "I'll drive you youngsters back to the campground. Going to bars is nothing new for me, so go ahead and get fucked up."

We all pat Rick on the back and tell him, "You're the man!"

Driving away from camp, Robert states, "I'm a 151 and Coke man."

"What? Have you ever even had one?" Fralia asks.

"Sure. That's what my mom drinks."

I ask, "Madge drinks 151 and Coke?"

"Yes."

Fralia jumps on it. "Well, well, well...I didn't know we had a mama's boy with us."

Robert looks in the rearview mirror, jaw clenched. "You say one thing about my mom, and I'll kill you. I don't care if you are Harris's friend."

"Okay, okay, guys. Geez, it's my birthday. Everyone lighten up."

It's quiet for too long. Then Robert puts in Grand Funk Railroad's "We're an American Band." Idaho is behind the times. Robert is carrying on like it's a brand-new song, singing at the top of his lungs, inserting "fucking" in front of "American band," and then going absolutely nuts about "four young chiquitas in Omaha." We are all laughing and singing with him.

"Rick, damn it! Rewind it! I need to hear it again," exclaims Robert.

We roll into town with all the windows down, singing "We're an American Band," while people stare at us. Robert parks in front of our first stop, The Wagon Wheel, and hurries into the bar. The three of us are still outside as Fralia gives his speech, taking delight in being my mentor.

"Okay, Harris. Here we go. Let me give you a few tips. First, hold your money like this when you're at the bar." He demonstrates with a five-dollar bill folded in half lengthwise. Rick shakes his head and chuckles. "Even though you're a new guy, don't act like one. Be polite to the bartender, make eye contact, and speak clearly. If we're lucky, there'll be a lady behind the bar, and you can watch me charm her. Order yourself a Singapore Sling."

As we walk through the swinging doors, Fralia nudges me. "Lady bartender. Just watch me. This is going to be fun," he says.

She's probably at least as old as our moms if she's a day old, but she's still a head turner, and no doubt she was absolutely stunning when she was younger—medium build, black hair, and piercing blue eyes. She has the healthy glow of someone who hasn't abused alcohol or drugs.

"Good evening," Fralia announces. "It's a beautiful day, and we're lucky to have a fine-looking lady behind the bar. All of that, and it's my best friend's eighteenth birthday. You'll be the lady he'll remember for the rest of his life—the one who poured him his first legal drink!"

She is smiling and no doubt humored by Fralia. "Your friend is a charming little devil, isn't he?" She winks. "My name is Wendy. Nice to meet you guys."

I don't know about the other two, but the wink did it for Fralia and me. It was code for *I'm confident and feisty.*

"The pleasure is all ours. I'm David. This is Robert, Rick, and the birthday boy is Gregory. Now, Gregory, you go first. Tell the beautiful lady what you'd like to drink."

"A Singapore Sling, please."

"Really? A Singapore Sling? You must be a sweet guy to like a sweet drink like that," replies Wendy.

I turn red.

"Sweetheart, put your money away. This one is on me. What would you other boys like?"

"151 and Coke," Robert says.

"Coors and a shot of Southern Comfort, please," Rick orders.

Smiling, Fralia says, "Jack. Neat. Two fingers, please."

Wendy squints at Fralia. "You charming little devil. If I were a few years younger, I'd let you charm the pants right off of me!"

And so it goes: Fralia and Wendy, bantering back and forth. She is toying with him, but he is up to the challenge and is able to hold his own. We have front-row seats to the great *Dave Fralia Show*. Robert even laughs a little.

The Singapore Sling is horrible—a bum steer by Fralia.

Wendy says, "Let's stick with gin, but go the opposite direction." She mixes me a gin and tonic. It is much more to my liking.

After about an hour, Robert starts getting antsy and tired of Fralia's act. He is ready to go to the next bar, and Robert—being Robert—isn't going to be quiet about wanting to leave. We are all buzzed but determined to hit all five bars. The next stop is off the main drag and must be the locals' bar. The place looks like a scene from a Bogart movie—everyone is smoking cigarettes. We can't get a seat at the bar, the vibe is bad, and there is no Wendy. The waitress cards us and doesn't say anything about it being my birthday. We all have a quick Coors and get out of the place.

At the third bar—Jake's—the bartender is a slow-moving old man. He'd probably be quicker if he weren't carrying around a ninety-pound bag of Portland cement for a belly. He finds no humor in us. Because the service is horrible, we start ordering two drinks each, so we don't have to wait so long.

Fralia starts grumbling about going back to see Wendy. I start thinking about all the money we are spending. How stupid—paying two dollars for a Coors, plus a tip, when we just bought a twelve-pack for $3.88.

Robert is getting really drunk. Under his breath, Fralia says, "That's what the dumbass gets for drinking 151." Rick sees Robert's behavior and tells us that any minute now Robert will turn into a mean, ugly drunk, and it won't be pretty.

He's seen it before, and he says to me, "We need to get out of here and back to camp before Robert picks a fight with someone. When he gets this fucked up, he's a complete dick."

Fralia whispers to me, "The guy's a complete dick all the time."

Rick has the keys and tells us all, "Time to leave, boys."

Fralia is lobbying for one last drink at The Wagon Wheel to see Wendy.

Robert starts slurring. "'Good afternoon, Your Honor. My name is David...David Warren Fralia. I'd like to plead guilty... with an explanation.'"

Fralia tells him, "You're drunk."

Robert slurs, "You're a pencil dick," and then he launches back into his impersonation.

"Let's go," I say.

Rick seconds it with "I'm the driver, and we're leaving."

We stumble out of the bar and amble down the block to the car.

Fralia tells Rick, "Harris and I are going to run in real quick and say goodbye to Wendy."

Rick turns around and says, "You've got two minutes. Then I'm firing up the engine and leaving."

We throw open the door to The Wagon Wheel. Wendy immediately sees us and smiles.

"It was great, Wendy, but we've got to leave," Fralia says. He then blows Wendy a kiss.

She smiles and tells us, "Don't break too many hearts."

The Idaho Falls boys can't resist being dicks and drive away when they see us coming out of the door. Then they stop, and when we get close, they take off again. They repeat it a couple more times, all the while giggling like little girls.

"Harris, tomorrow can't get here soon enough. I don't want to see this Robert guy ever again."

"I hear you," is all I can say.

The last thing we need when we get back to camp is the first thing we do—drink more Coors. Being away from people and the town, the beer just makes us tired. We light a small fire but let it quickly die. Fralia and I get into our two-man tent. The Idaho Falls boys sleep in the Firebird.

As the sun rises, everyone wakes up and pisses. Robert fires up his Firebird. He then says, "Happy birthday," and they drive off.

"He wants to go home to see his mama," Fralia says, shaking his head.

"I don't know what to say."

"Well, I do." I can see Fralia mentally getting up on his soapbox. "You may have been a kid when you met him in Sacramento, and I get playing around with him in sixth, seventh, and eighth grade, but you're eighteen now. That guy has a screw loose, and there's hatred in his heart. You need to disassociate with him. He's bad news."

"Well, we've invited him to San Diego, and you promised him Shelly."

"That was stupid. Hopefully, he'll forget."

"He won't forget. Trust me. He never forgets anything," I tell him.

"We'll cross that bridge when the time comes. Now let's cook some breakfast, inventory our beer, and get out of here."

"Better yet—let's break camp, go to town, and have a big-ass breakfast at the diner. Then hit the store and skedaddle," I say.

"Good idea."

"And by the way, we only have two beers left," I say, knowing it would get him excited.

"Dammit!"

We are starving, probably hung over, and eat like horses. Fralia is drinking coffee like he is some middle-aged man. I just don't understand this whole coffee-drinking thing.

"Let's pool our money together. It'll be easier to manage," Fralia says between coffee sips.

Amazingly enough, we still have $450 left. Damn, that's a lot of money, and we both agree that should easily get us four weeks on the road and back to San Diego. Shit, in nine days, we have only spent a $150 at the big-money stops.

"Let's go get some more ice and some $3.88 twelve-packs of Coors," I say.

"Okay. Let's also think about our next few stops and what we'll be eating," says Fralia, sounding like an adult.

"This has always been the loose part of the trip. I'm proposing we leave here and head over to Salmon, then the Stanley area—basically the middle of nowhere. We'll move when our supplies get low and we need to replenish. I also see us eating a lot of trout and rabbit."

"Okay, Jeremiah Johnson. Let's bust out the map, and show me the route. As you know, this is all virgin territory to me. Let's figure out the mileage between stops."

"Good idea. We don't want to run out of gas in the middle of nowhere. I want to call my mom before we leave town. And let's try to call Pat Acomb."

We shop, gas up, and use the phone booth at the Sinclair gas station. I call my mom collect and tell her what she wants to hear about my birthday night—basically a pack of lies. Fralia tells his mother the same lies, more or less.

"Okay, Harris. Let's call Acomb. Are you ready?"

"Yup."

"If his mom answers, should I call her MJ or Mrs. Acomb?" Fralia wonders.

"Dude, I'm the only one that can get away with calling her MJ," I say.

"Okay, here we go." Fralia dials zero and states, "Operator, I'd like to make a long-distance call and charge it to my home phone."

Barely audible, the operator says, "Your name and home phone, please."

"Clark. Zach Clark. 714-748-0821," Fralia says.

I do my best not to laugh. Poor Zach is always getting picked on.

"And the number you'd like to call?"

"714-484-0921."

"Hello?"

"Mrs. Acomb?" he asks.

"Who's this?" she says.

"David Fralia."

"What do you want, you little shit?"

"I'm here with Harris. Can we talk to Pat?"

"Where's here?"

"Montana."

"Why are you in Montana?" she asks.

"Give me the phone," I say to Fralia. "MJ, it's Greg. Is Pat there?" I say into the phone.

"Patrick! Get in here, dammit. The phone is for you. It's one of your little boyfriends."

"Hello?"

"Acomb!"

"Ha! You guys haven't killed each other yet?"

"Not even," I say.

"Well, let's hear all about it."

"Okay, here's Fralia."

Fralia turns on his glib switch and starts stretching the truth. Acomb, knowing Fralia is being Fralia, just lets him roll, but, basically, it all really happened.

MIDDLE OF NOWHERE, IDAHO

"So, Fralia, what's your take on this new guy, Tom Petty?"

"Well, I love the name Heartbreakers, but I don't know. 'American Girl' I like, but 'Breakdown' is too slow."

"Have you listened to all of it?" I want to know.

"Yeah, I've heard it a few times. Did you bring it?"

"No. I only have the album and was out of blank tapes, so I couldn't record it. But like usual, the best song on the album isn't getting any airplay."

"What song?" he asks.

"Fourth song, side one. 'The Wild One, Forever.'"

"I don't think the guy is going to amount to anything. Peter Frampton is the one who's going to have a huge career."

"You think?" I say.

"Hell, yes! Chicks absolutely dig him. *Frampton Comes Alive!* is huge. The guy is a chick magnet. But right now, it's time for a little *Fly Like an Eagle*."

"Dude. Really? Again? Christ, we have over a hundred tapes, and you want to hear that again?" I say, exasperated.

"It's a masterpiece. I love it. I can't get enough of it. Right from the start, 'Space Intro' grabs me. It's great."

"But we've already heard it at least twenty times," I implore.

"So?"

"Do me a favor, and give Steve Miller a rest for at least a day."

"Okay, Gregory. I'll blindly pick a tape out of your case. Drum roll please...and the winner is...America! How does a little 'Sister Golden Hair' sound?"

"Absolutely refreshing."

There are always highs and lows. Without the lows, how do you appreciate the highs? Our low is the halfway point of the trip. The romance of being in the middle of nowhere is wearing off. It's just us, getting bored and tired of each other's company. We are also homesick—missing our family and friends and the San Diego weather, but interestingly enough, not our girlfriends.

There's no beach in Idaho, but there are plenty of mosquitoes. I warned Fralia about the mosquitoes, but when we arrive in the Salmon area, they are really bad. While setting up camp, the Cutter repellent isn't protecting us at all. We are getting the living shit bitten out of us. There are only two places to take refuge: Herman and the two-man tent. I take Herman, and Fralia goes into the two-man tent. So we have relief from the mosquitoes and each other, but it isn't fun.

The blue sky quickly turns dark, and the air is dead calm. *Crack!*

The thunder scares the bejesus out of me. "Fralia, are you all right?" I yell toward the tent.

The rain is coming down like it's the end of the world. A bolt lights up the dark sky, and the thunder immediately sounds.

"Yes," he replies.

"Jesus Christ! Get out of that tent and get over here before you get zapped."

He runs the short distance to Herman and jumps into the passenger seat, soaking wet. We crack the windows and bust out laughing.

"We're not in San Diego anymore," I say in jest.

"No fucking shit. Unfortunately, we're a long way from San Diego."

"The good news is this storm has cleared out the mosquitoes. Let's see what tomorrow brings," I say, trying to keep Fralia calm.

"What it's going to bring is us getting the fuck out of here! You think the mosquitoes are going to disappear? You're nuts."

"You're probably right, but we'll see," I say. "Since you're already wet, why don't you run outside and grab the cooler? I'll get the cigarette lighter glowing. Time for a Garcia y Vega and a Coors!"

"Great idea, Gregory."

We sit in Herman, smoke cigars, and drink Coors. We don't play any of our cassettes for fear of running down the battery. Instead, we sing REO's "Ridin' the Storm Out."

Two hours and the rain is not letting up. So we have dinner in Herman: a can of Pringles, Ritz crackers, Tillamook cheddar, and a box of Fiddle Faddle. We have a great time, laugh a lot, and drink until all the Coors are gone. It's still raining, but after four hours of sitting in Herman, we are ready for the tent.

"Fralia, you run over there first, and tell me if the inside of the tent is wet. If it is, I'm staying in Herman."

"Okay, pussy."

"Run! Run, you slow fucker!" I yell at Fralia while pushing him out his open door.

"Ha, Harris! Believe it or not, it's dry in here!" Fralia laughs as he crawls inside the tent.

"Okay, clear out. Here I come!" I say.

We wake up to a clear, cold morning. There's no waiting around to see what the day will bring. We break camp and flee the Salmon area. Destination: Redfish Lake.

"Do you know how many Coors we have left?" Fralia wonders.

"Are you kidding? We drank them all last night."

"Really?"

"Yeah, really. You were pounding them," I say.

"Really? We drank them all?"

"Geez, I can't believe you don't remember. And apparently, we're no Jeremiah Johnsons. Kind of pathetic a few mosquitoes chase us away," I tell him.

"A few mosquitoes, my ass. And fuck Jeremiah Johnson. This is 1978, not 1850. Mankind is more intelligent now. You have to be stupid to stay and get the shit bitten out of you. Besides, they probably had some trick back then like rubbing elk piss all over your body or maybe bear shit. I've never seen so many mosquitoes in my life. What is it about Salmon?"

"Can't say. Just hoping Redfish Lake is better," I respond.

"It better be," he says, "or we'll just keep on driving. So far, the best thing I can say about your middle-of-nowhere Idaho is they'd probably sell beer to a twelve-year-old. Speaking of beer…stop at the first place that sells it since you drank it all last night."

Fucking Fralia, I think to myself. "Okay, don't worry. We'll get more beer. The last time I was at Redfish Lake, we slayed the Dolly Varden trout. It'll be trout for dinner again. And maybe you can wash your hair in the lake. It's looking like the Santa Barbara oil spill."

"I don't know what it looks like, but I can tell you, it smells like grease. And when we get back to San Diego, I'm never eating trout again. You can have everything I catch at Lake Poway."

"I'm feeling good about Redfish Lake," I tell Fralia.

REDFISH LAKE

We roll in before noon on Thursday to a smattering of campers and snag a beautiful lakefront spot.

"See, Fralia? I told you I had a good feeling about Redfish. Now, let's get set up, jump into the lake, and bathe. I can't wait to see the oil slick from your hair."

"Don't think you don't stink, too, because you do!"

We strip off our clothes—then into the lake we go. Damn, it's nice to be clean. We both feel great. The mosquitoes are manageable, the sky's blue, and there's no threat of rain. After dinner, we wet our lines and slay the trout.

"Fuck Salmon, Idaho, Harris."

"Yeah, that wasn't really fun."

"It sucked. I was ready to throw in the towel and drive straight home."

"There's always tomorrow," I say in a role reversal, trying to be the positive one.

"Well, if *this* tomorrow is like yesterday, then tomorrow, we'd be home."

"Well, it ain't. Let's see what kind of folks show up for the weekend. Maybe you can find someone to talk to besides me!"

"I should only be so lucky," Fralia grumbles.

◆ ◆ ◆

Friday afternoon, the weekend warriors start to roll in. I'm tidying up Herman after the mess we left in her during our rainstorm dinner at Salmon. Meanwhile, Fralia has dumped a cup of noodles by our campfire grill, trying to lure in some chipmunks so he can snap their picture. We are both content not talking to each other—that is, until our neighbors arrive.

"Psst! Fralia, get over here."

"What?"

"Now. Quick!" I say.

"All right, all right."

"Look what's setting up next to us."

"Oh my God," he says. "She's a stone-cold fox."

"Ya think?"

"Oh my God!" he repeats himself. "You were right about Redfish Lake. Hands down the hottest chick of the whole trip. Maybe the hottest chick ever."

"How old do you think she is?" I ask.

"Twenty-eight to thirty-two. Those two little kids are hers. I'm guessing five and seven years old. And that dork is her husband."

"How does that work?" I say, completely puzzled.

"Good question! She's way out of that guy's league. He must have money. Damn," Fralia says. "She's perfect. I'm saying five feet, five inches, maybe one hundred twenty-five pounds, perfect breasts, tight little ass, natural blonde, and tan all over. She's like Farrah Fawcett's better-looking sister. Way hotter than any *Charlie's Angel*."

"Is she hot because we haven't seen any chicks for shit...or is she hot?"

"What?" Fralia asks. "She's smoking hot, Harris. For God's sake, look at her. Have you ever seen a better ass in a pair of Dittos? And how about that tube top? Are you kidding me? Look at her."

"I am, but now her husband is looking over here."

Hubby is a stoop-shouldered version of a younger Bob Newhart. His stomach is more than a bit flabby, and he's going bald.

"Okay. Let's play it cool. Go about our business...let them set up. Then we'll introduce ourselves."

"You're the glib one," I tell him. "I'll follow your lead."

We putz around and do our best to check her out without getting caught. Once they get their camper level and unloaded, Fralia says, "Okay, Gregory. Here we go." He leaves my side and traipses confidently over to the happy couple. *Classic Fralia*, I'm thinking as I follow him.

"Howdy, neighbors," he says.

"Hello, guys," says the blonde we've been drooling over.

"How long are you here?" Fralia asks.

"Just the weekend," she tells us. "Honey, come over here and meet our neighbors," she calls to her husband.

"I'm David," Fralia says. He then nods his head in my direction. "This is Gregory."

"Hi boys. I'm Mr. Hilker." He gives us a wimpy handshake.

"Guys, you can call me AJ," says the sexy blonde, who is even hotter up close. She tells her two towheaded kids to come over and introduce themselves.

"Hi," the younger boy says. "I'm Joe."

"I'm Jackie," says the older one. "Do you guys fish?"

"Ha," says Fralia. "Do we fish? Gregory is the champion of Lake Poway."

"Lake Poway?" asks AJ. "Where's that?"

"San Diego," replies Fralia.

"You guys are from San Diego?" AJ says. "I've always wanted to go there!"

One thing we've found out on this trip is that being from California is a big thing, and being from San Diego is even bigger. Just the words "San Diego" elicit admiration. "Lucky!" people reply. "Oh my God! I love it there!" they exclaim. "You've got the best weather," they admire. And some people actually ask us if we know Joan Embery. Just for fun, Fralia sometimes says, "Yes," and then tells them she is as nice in person as she is on *The Tonight Show*.

"We sure are," Fralia says to AJ. "Gregory and I are just on a little summer tour of the western states."

Jackie tugs on his mom's arm. "Can we fish with them?" he whispers.

"You have to ask your dad...and David and Gregory," AJ tells him. "Plus, I don't remember them inviting you."

Fralia sees his opening and seizes it. "Boys, first thing in the morning, we'll fish. Right there in front of our site."

Jackie and Joe turn to their father. "Dad, please?" they ask together.

"All right, boys."

"Yay!" the two boys shout.

AJ smiles and says, "I'll tell you what. If you guys catch enough trout, I'll cook us all dinner tomorrow night."

I say, "It's a done deal."

"Okay," says Fralia. "Have a great evening, and we'll see you in the morning."

As we stroll back to our site, Fralia pinches me and whispers, "Oh my God. Did you see her?"

"Yeah. I fucking saw her. She's hot."

"She's the complete package. I've seen too many beauties who have the personality of a rock. She doesn't."

The next morning, we find out why the kids were so excited to fish with us. Their dad doesn't fish.

We just can't figure this guy out—living in Boise, married to no doubt the hottest chick in the state, two boys, and he doesn't fish. We're perplexed. What is wrong with this guy?

AJ and Mr. Hilker are sitting on their picnic table, watching their boys. The kids have some piece-of-shit Zebco rods and reels with crappy line that will only cast a few yards.

We quickly decide not to use their setups. Instead, we let them use ours to give them a real learning experience with good equipment. The boys are wide-eyed and eager to learn.

"Okay, guys," I say. "First, we're going to wake up the fish with some Mepps lures. Joe, you can use my rod, but I'll cast it for you. Jackie, David will help you cast. On these types of reels, you open the bale, put your finger right here on the line, point the tip of the rod behind you, and keep the reel even with your shoulder. Then you cast like this." I bring my arm around, and with a quick snap of the wrist, I let it rip and drop it right on top of the honey hole. "Reel it in about this speed." Right when I start cranking the reel...*Bam!*

"Hook up!" I scream, scaring everyone except Fralia, who's used to fishing with me.

I hand the rod to Joe. He's reeling and yelling, "Mom! Mom!"

AJ and Mr. Hilker come down to the shoreline. She's smiling, and her blue eyes are twinkling like Sirius.

Joe reels the fish in. I unhook it for him, put it on the stringer, and hand it to him. He's all smiles as he holds up the stringer. AJ uses her little Kodak Instamatic camera to take a picture of Joe and me.

Fralia grins and says, "What time is dinner, AJ?"

Jackie rips four on his own, and Joe gets a couple more with my help. Then it just dies. So I decide it's time to switch gears. We show the boys how to set up an egg sinker with an eighteen-inch leader on two-pound test. I bust into a fresh jar of Zeke's yellow floating bait and tell the kids to be careful putting the cheese on the triple-prong hook of death.

We let Joe cast his rod this time, show the boys how to make the line tight, and set the rods on a log. We tell them to stand in front of the rods and when they see the tip move, grab the rod, set the hook, and yell, "Hook up!"

We don't know where Mr. Hilker is, but AJ comes down and chats us up. She wants to hear stories about our trip and San Diego. The fishing is steady, and at one point, we have a double hookup with both boys yelling, "Hook up! Hook up!"

The five of us are laughing. AJ is grateful for our patience with her kids. She is one special lady.

Even though we are fishing without licenses, we stop when we hit our limits and tell the boys that now it's time to clean the fish. We show them the proper way to do it. We explain that first you take a sharp knife and slit the trout from anus to throat. Then separate the gills from the head with the knife. Pull firmly down on the gills to remove them along with the accompanying guts. And finally, use your thumbnail to remove the remaining dark-colored blood sac along the backbone. At first, they are a little squeamish, but their mom insists they do it themselves. "You've had your fun time," she tells them, mussing their hair with her hand. "Now you have to do the hard work."

We give AJ all the cleaned fish. "Come on over at four," she says. "We'll eat around five. I'll have some cold beers for you guys. I really can't thank you two enough. My boys had the time of their lives."

Once AJ and the boys are beyond hearing range, Fralia announces, "I'm in love."

"Oh, Fralia."

"I'm in love. She's one of a kind. Most beauties only stay on the pedestal when viewed from afar, but once you talk to them and get to know them, their beauty diminishes. Not AJ. She's even better now."

"And married with two kids."

"Yeah, yeah," he acknowledges. "Nothing wrong with fantasizing."

"True. Just behave at dinner."

We do nothing but count down the minutes to four o'clock. When we walk over, she reaches into the cooler, pulls out two Coors, pops them open, and hands us each one.

We may be young and sometimes slow, but I swear she's flirting with both of us. She tells us she's going to come to San Diego to visit if we promise to take her to the beach.

"Sure, no problem," Fralia says. He takes a long gulp of his beer. "That would be great." He's outwardly beaming with confidence, but I know he's shitting bricks.

Mr. Hilker is even less of a talker than I am. He keeps a close watch on both of us, but mostly on Fralia. My sense is he knows his wife is sexy and that her talkative, friendly nature is often confused with flirting, but I still think she's flirting.

Fralia just can't help himself from being Fralia. During dinner, he turns on his charm.

"AJ, I thought I was tired of trout because we've eaten so much of it the last two weeks. But this"—he points his fork at the fish on his plate—"is fantastic. I don't know what your trick is, but I wish you'd show Gregory here because his trout doesn't taste anything like this."

"Oh, David. You're so kind. Did you hear that, kids?" she says, turning to her two sons. "David is a polite young man. This is exactly how you boys should be—appreciative. Girls like that."

After dinner, Mr. Hilker wraps things up and sends us on our way. Too bad because Fralia is just getting warmed up.

Back at camp, Fralia says, "That guy is a dick."

"Christ. You were practically drooling all over his wife."

"The guy is a dick. Wimpy handshake, glasses, belly, and balding."

"He's a dick with a smokin' hot wife," I say.

"But a dick nonetheless."

It's still light out, but the Hilkers retire for the night.

"Show's over, Fralia," I say. "The love of your life just went into her camper with her dick of a husband and two kids. Ha, ha."

"Goddamn." He can't let it go. "She's hot...foxiest lady ever. I bet she's in her sexual prime and would love a young stud like me!"

I look across at him doubtfully. "Young stud, huh?"

"That's right. I would make her scream my name."

"Okay, that's enough," I inform him. "I don't want you lying next to me and jacking off."

"Yeah, yeah, yeah, but I bet I have a wet dream about AJ tonight."

The next morning, the Hilkers break camp to head back to Boise. Much to the chagrin of Mr. Hilker, Fralia volunteers to help them pack up. I have no doubt, if not for us, he would have stayed until the afternoon. The boys thank us, but Mr. Hilker does not shake our hands.

AJ, however, gives both of us hugs.

And then…they are gone.

"Did you feel her hug, Harris?"

"Are you kidding? Damn."

"Goddamn is more like it. I mean, wow! She is hot!"

"And now nothing more than a memory."

"One I won't forget. Well, shit. No AJ, so let's blow this Popsicle stand," says a downhearted Fralia.

"Might as well. Let's jump in the lake and get cleaned up first. Then head for Oregon."

Before taking off, we put the recycled oil back into Herman, and I wonder how long I'm going to have to listen to Fralia fantasize about AJ.

OREGON

I just can't help myself and tell Fralia, "I want you to wave to AJ as we drive by Boise."

"What a dick. Do you realize we didn't even get a picture of her? No one's going to believe how hot she was," says Fralia.

"She was smokin' hot," I say.

"Time for a little Steve Miller, *Fly Like an Eagle*!"

"Christ, again?" I say. "It was a good album, but you've ruined it. Playing it over and over! You're worse than KCBQ. I'd like to put a moratorium on *Fly Like an Eagle*. If I hear it one more time, I'm throwing it out the window."

"Geez. That's a little over the top. Just chill. I'll tell you what. I'll stop playing *Fly Like an Eagle* if you stop playing that whiny Neil Young *Harvest*. Every time I hear it, I can't get Coach Self out of my mind," says Fralia.

Perplexed, I say, "Coach Self? What the hell does Coach Self have to do with *Harvest*?"

"Don't you remember when we had weightlifting for athletic PE our sophomore year? Coach dragged in a turntable and some shitty speakers and played that album over and over while we were doing circuit training. He would bark at whoever was closest to flip the album after the side was over."

"I hate lifting weights. I think I blocked that out of my mind," I utter.

"Well, I can't get it out of my mind."

"I have an idea. Why don't we try silence?" I tell him.

So silence it is, but that just makes the tension in the VW worse. It's so thick, you can cut it with a pocketknife. I start feeling bad about threatening to throw the tape out the window. Finally, after half an hour, I relent.

"Okay. Put in *Fly Like an Eagle*. Anything is better than this silence."

"You're right. Then after that, *Harvest*. Fuck Coach Self."

For what seems like the millionth time, I listen to "Space Intro" lead into "Fly Like an Eagle," followed by the rest of side one of the tape. Then we flip it over and play side two—a total of thirty-eight minutes of listening to Fralia trying to sing like Steve Miller.

We give ourselves three days to get to Astoria. From there, our plan is to take the 101 all the way down the Oregon coast and into California.

We are both kind of surprised. We assumed Oregon would be all pine trees and mountains, but it isn't. The eastern half is high desert.

We drive on Interstate 84 until we hit the Columbia River, and then we pass a blip on the road called Rufus and cross into Washington. Originally, we hadn't planned to go into Washington, but we decide to go ahead and hit another state.

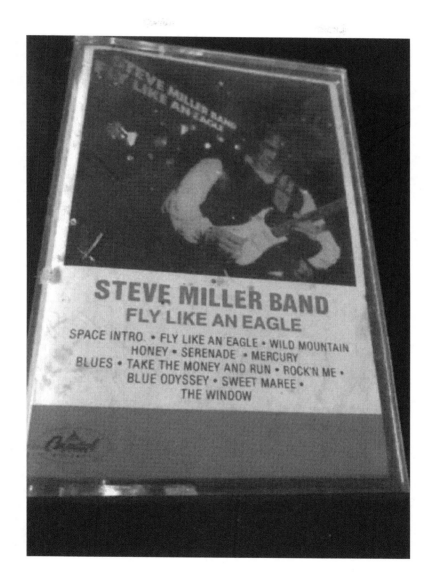

We set up camp at Avery Recreation Area. The view of Mount Adams to the northwest and Mount Hood to the southwest is unbelievable—much like two hot chicks that we can't keep our eyes off of. It's just as mesmerizing as the Tetons.

"Can you imagine if one of these volcanoes blew its top?" Fralia says.

"Dude. You have an active imagination."

"I do!" Fralia agrees.

"It'll never happen," I claim.

Little did we know, two years later, Mount Saint Helens would blow, killing fifty-seven people and destroying hundreds of homes and miles of roads and railway.

"Come look at the map, Fralia, since you're driving the first leg tomorrow. We'll cross back into Oregon on 197 and then get back on I-84. When we hit Portland, we'll get off the interstate and get on Highway 30 to get to Astoria and the 101. I kind of want to see the Columbia dump into the Pacific. And look what's a few towns south of Astoria. Tillamook!"

"No shit. Like the cheese? Hot damn. Let's check that out," Fralia says with excitement.

"There are campgrounds all along the coastline. We'll just pick one close to Tillamook and check out the scene for a couple of days, then continue down the coastline to the Golden State."

"There's got to be some kind of cheese factory. I can't wait to see it."

"You know I'm a big cheese guy!" I respond.

It was so youthful of us to continue looking forward to the next thing instead of living in the moment.

"Time to tally up our cash. Count it out for me, Fralia."

"Okay. Notice I have all the bills facing the same direction. That's how you stack your money. Denominations together and all facing the same direction," states Fralia as though he's a bank teller.

"Okay, okay. How much do we have?" I'm dying to know.

"More than enough, I bet."

"Count!"

"Two hundred fifty dollars. I told you in Jackson Hole not to worry about it," says Fralia.

"Looks like you were right. Down the coast, Sacramento, San Jose, then home sweet home. Probably less than two weeks."

The next day, we don't have the gumption to jump back into Herman. So we just spend another day doing a lot of nothing except talking about AJ and staring at Mount Hood and Mount Adams.

There's a pay phone at the campground entrance, so we make calls to my Aunt Dot and David Hoime, my best friend in Sacramento, to give them the heads up we'll be there in two to three days. This time, instead of charging it to someone else's home phone, we pay for the calls with the loose change we have been collecting.

The next day, we depart late for Tillamook, somehow get lost in Portland, and can't find Highway 30. We are both blaming each other, and we get all stressed and pissy. We finally right the ship and find our way. The Columbia River pouring into the Pacific is amazing. We both can't believe how wide the mouth is and comment on how it's good to see the Pacific again. We hang a left and start going south on the 101.

Tillamook is a bust. Just the name Tillamook holds a mythical status in our minds, but the cheese factory smells horrible, and we both agree we would've been better off never seeing it. Now we think less of the name. Some things are definitely best left unknown and unseen.

Getting lost in Portland and experiencing the disillusionment of Tillamook puts a dark cloud over everything. So we decide to skip camping in Tillamook, drive to Lincoln City, and look for a place to have dinner. We stop at a greasy spoon with an amazing ocean view.

Our late start begins to haunt us. It's misty out, and it's getting dark earlier than we expected. After dinner, we decide to push on a little farther to Dunes City. Our full stomachs make us tired. We put in Van Halen, hoping it will pump us up, but travel fatigue is setting in. Herman seems to be getting smaller. We are tired of all our cassette tapes and definitely tired of each other.

The week before, we were so pumped about the Oregon 101 section of the trip. But now it's dark, and we don't know where we'll be camping at Dunes City, so we keep pushing on. A dense fog begins to roll in, and Fralia is driving.

"Did you see that?" yells Fralia as he turns down the volume.

"No. What was it? I was nodding off," I say.

"It was some Jesus Christ-looking guy in a white flowing robe with long hair walking on the shoulder."

"Should we stop?" I ask.

"Hell, no!" Fralia shouts.

"Are you sure?"

"Hell, yes. I'm sure we shouldn't stop," says Fralia.

"No...are you sure you *saw* someone?"

"I'm pretty sure," replies Fralia.

Then around the next twisty turn, there are two hippie-looking chicks in white flowing robes.

"What the hell?" I say.

Suddenly, there are three more white robe-wearing nuts out in the pitch dark walking the side of the road. Neither of us is going to admit it, but we are both scared.

At the same time, we both say, "Let's get out of this place!"

We decide to get off the 101 as soon as we can and get over to the I-5.

Two hours later, at midnight, we arrive in Roseburg via Highway 42. It's the most tired we have been the whole trip. We sleep in Herman at a rest area. We awake at sunrise to fogged windows and people staring in at us.

Today, we will be in Sacramento with other people to talk to—thank God—and we'll be sleeping in my aunt's house...in separate rooms!

Looking back now, it's easy to see we were getting sick of each other's company.

SACRAMENTO

My dad's side of the family is interesting, to say the least. I didn't even meet my real paternal grandmother until I was twelve. The whole time I thought this other lady, who I didn't like at all, was my real grandmother. No one told me any different. My dad has a lot of half brothers and sisters. I can't count them all, nor have I met them all. But my Aunt Dot is my dad's full sibling. Growing up in Sacramento, Aunt Dot, Uncle Gib, and my two cousins, Kahl and Ty, were just a few miles away on the other side of the American River in Carmichael. We'd see them all the time.

I fill Fralia in on the background. "Dot and Gib are divorced. I've been told it was a messy divorce. Ty, who's my brother's age, is still at home. I'm not certain where Kahl is. He's a little older than us. What I want to warn you about is Dot is a neat freak. I'll show you a room we shouldn't even walk into. Don't dick around with anything. Take your shoes off, and don't make a mess."

"Don't worry, Harris. I just want to take a shower and sleep in a bed."

We drive across the Watt Avenue Bridge, and I point out the American River. "We'll be floating down that bad boy tomorrow."

We pull up to Aunt Dot's house on Saint James Drive and park on the street so we don't leave a lake of oil on her driveway. I'm worried, however, about the mess we might make on the street.

"Hurry, Fralia. Get that oil-catching container under the engine. If we leave an oil puddle on her street, Dot will shit."

It's a beautiful, single-level, early '60s house. It still looks like a model home with a perfectly manicured lawn. Aunt Dot and Ty hear us pull up and come out to greet us. It's nice to be greeted. They are both happy to see us and excited to hear some stories from the road.

Just as I described, Aunt Dot is still a neat freak, but Fralia turns on his charm, follows the rules, and my aunt loves him, just like my mom loves him…like every parent loves him.

Dot makes us a great home-cooked meal of spaghetti, garlic bread, and salad. Fralia loves garlic bread, especially when it's dripping with butter, so he is really stoked. During dinner, we tell them about the littering ticket, seeing a bald eagle in the Tetons, and my birthday night. We save the AJ story for later when we can tell only Ty. After dinner, Aunt Dot lets me use her phone—but only after I wash my hands. I call David Hoime to confirm we are all set for floating the American River tomorrow. He tells me we will meet in front of the Safeway at one o'clock. He has all the tubes, rafts, and coolers, and he will be bringing a couple of friends. And the best news—his older brother will buy us beers.

"Just be sure you guys have lunch! Don't show up with an empty stomach," Hoime says.

Before we go to bed, we hang out in Ty's room and listen to music, mostly Elton John's, *Captain Fantastic and The Brown Dirt Cowboy*. Ty really loves "Someone Saved My Life Tonight."

"So where's Kahl?" I ask.

"I don't know for sure, but I'll track him down. He's not getting along with Dot, but I'm sure he'll come over to see you," Ty says.

"He's not at your dad's?"

"Sometimes he is, sometimes he isn't."

Dot knocks on the door and tells us, "Music off."

So we go to our separate rooms.

It's been over three weeks since we've slept in a bed. With full bellies, a roof over our heads, and nice beds, we sleep like rocks. Our sleep is so sound, we don't get up until ten in the morning. By then, Dot is at work. Ty is still at home. He's in the backyard, looking for something.

"Good morning, cousin," Ty says.

"Good morning, cousin," I repeat. "What are you looking for?"

"I'm trying to find that damn tortoise."

"Dude. You guys still have that thing?" I say.

"Maybe. I haven't seen it in a while."

"What can we have for breakfast?" I ask.

"Help yourself to anything you want," he says. "Just be sure you clean up and don't leave a mess. You know how my mom is."

"Ten-four that," I say.

"Oh hey, I tracked down my brother, he'll be here tomorrow morning."

"Right on!"

Fralia cooks us a couple of big omelets, and we drink real orange juice. I think I might actually prefer Tang. We've had it just about every morning, and I've grown accustomed to it.

"Let's turn on the TV," says Fralia.

"Okay, but don't sit on the furniture," I say.

"What a trip. That's the exact Zenith TV we have at home," he says.

We check all six channels. There's nothing on for shit except an old *Wild Wild West* rerun that we've both seen.

"Too bad there's not a *Rockford Files* on. I can watch those reruns all day long," I say.

"Jimmy, Jimmy," Fralia says.

"Nice Angel impersonation," I say.

"Thanks. I love that character. Is that omelet going to hold you?"

"No way, dude," I say. "Let's go to Der Wienerschnitzel and get some corn dogs before meeting Hoime."

"Let's do it!"

After we each take down three corn dogs, we head over to the Safeway. We arrive a little early, so we wait at the back of the lot.

"There he is," I tell Fralia. "He's driving that tan Datsun truck."

He sees us and pulls up next to Herman.

"Hey, Hoime."

"Hey, Harris," Hoime says. "Goddamn, it's good to see you."

"The same." We shake hands. "This is my friend, Dave Fralia."

"Nice to meet you," Hoime says. "You remember Mark and Jeff, right?"

"Of course. Good to see you guys again."

Everyone shakes hands. The three Sacramento guys are in cutoff jeans, and we are wearing our Birdwell Beach Britches. No one is going to mistake us for locals.

"My brother bought us a couple cases of Oly," Hoime says. "I hope that's good."

"It'll work. We're usually Coors guys, but cold beer is cold beer," I say.

"Okay, follow us," Hoime says. "We'll leave your Bug at the takeout."

We follow Hoime to the takeout spot at Geothe Park, park Herman, and jump into the bed of the truck with the coolers and deflated tubes and rafts. Excited, we reach into a cooler and each grab an Oly to drink on the way to the launch. The launch is on Sunrise Boulevard, across the street from a Mobil gas station, where we inflate everything. It's only ninety degrees—a cool day for Sacramento in July.

Hoime gives us the safety talk before launching.

"Okay, we'll be floating for close to three hours. It's mellow except for the San Juan Rapids and some wood debris and plants we need to maneuver around by the Gilligan's Island sandbar. I'll sweep just to make sure we don't get too separated or run into any problems. And put your empties back into the cooler. You San Diego boys have a good time!"

Instead of D Street in Encinitas, this is what the Sac kids do: float the American River. And just like D Street, it doesn't disappoint. Hot, tan chicks looking to get tanner and have fun are all over the place.

Jeff and I grab a couple of tubes and a cooler and are the first to launch. Mark is behind us. Fralia is dicking around on the shore doing God knows what, and Hoime is patiently waiting for him. Quite a few groups launched farther upstream and float by as we enter. Jeff seems to know most of them.

We are only in the water for a few minutes, when Jeff says, "There are four Johnson High chicks coming up on us. Let's slow down our tubes and let them catch up. Then we'll tie up to their raft."

"Hi, Jeff. Who's your friend?" the cutest girl flirtingly wants to know.

"Come on over and tie up, and I'll introduce you." Jeff gives me a little head nod.

"Okay," she says.

"Girls, this is Greg Harris," Jeff says. "He's an old friend of Hoime's. They go all the way back to Sequoia Elementary School."

"Hi, Greg," they all say.

They each introduce themselves: Nicole, Danny, Tamara, and Barb. They are all wearing board shorts and bikini tops, and they are oiled up with Hawaiian Tropic. All four of them are flirts and cute, but Danny is hot. How could she not be when she is going by the name Danny? She's tall and athletic with dirty-blond hair in a ponytail. Her sparkling green eyes are hypnotizing.

"You girls want a beer?" Jeff asks.

They all say, "Please!"

"So Greg lives in San Diego now," Jeff tells them.

"Lucky!" they all say in unison.

Barb is staring at me. "I swear I know you. Did you have Mrs. Jones in third grade?"

"Geez. I can't remember, but Hoime and I were in the same class."

"So was I!" Barb says excitedly.

I have no idea who this chick is, but I play along, and it gives me an opportunity to really look at her. Finally, I say, "Oh, yeah, I remember you."

Then she says, "I think your brother and my sister were in the same kindergarten class."

"Could be," I say. "Do you remember a guy named Robert James?"

"No, it doesn't ring a bell."

"He moved in the second grade. My buddy and I just visited him in Idaho a few weeks ago."

"Really? You were in Idaho?" Danny asks.

"Yes, we're touring the western states. This is the tail end of our trip."

Danny is putting on the charm. "Wow, you're so lucky! The four of us are stuck in Sacramento all summer."

"Well, let me tell you, your tans look great!" I say.

It's fun flirting. I'm good at it, but Fralia is a master. Too bad he's not tied up with us. Together, we have great fun, but we are loyal to our girlfriends, so it never goes beyond flirting.

I felt like a dope when I learned a week after we got back to San Diego that my chick cheated on me the whole time we were gone.

We all chitchat for a while. Danny is definitely the leader of the group. Barb is her sidekick, and Tamara and Nicole are just extras in the little play they are putting on for Jeff and me.

I learn Danny and Hoime were a thing their sophomore year. We talk about the fall. Tamara and Nicole will both be going to Chico State, and Barb will attend American River College.

Danny arches her back and says, "I'm going to UCLA on an athletic scholarship for volleyball."

"Of course, you are. That's the least surprising thing I've heard all summer," I say to all of them.

It's quite a pleasant afternoon, and a bit strange not being attached to the guy I've been sharing oxygen with the last four weeks. I even take a little floating nap—that is, until the chicks start putting ice cubes in my belly button. They are all laughing and quite pleased with themselves.

Next thing I know, three delightful hours have passed, and it's time to exit the river. The four chicks take off in a station wagon but not before asking Jeff if they'll be at Sunrise tonight. He tells them, "Probably."

Jeff and I sit on the shore waiting for the rest of our group and watch all the pretties float by. Most of them wave to Jeff. We start talking about the future. Jeff moved to Sacramento a year before I moved. We remember each other but not well. He's one of those red-headed guys who are able to tan. He is also a stud athlete—a three-sport star: southpaw pitcher, power forward, and quarterback. Football is his passion. Unfortunately, his grades were low because having fun was a priority. So his plan is to go to American River College, play football, and transfer into a Division I program with two years of eligibility. I tell him that Fralia and I are also going to a junior college.

"There's Mark," says Jeff. "Hoime and your buddy must be close." Jeff then shouts, "Hey, Mark! Where are the other two guys?"

"Good question. I haven't seen them since right after we launched," says Mark.

"Fuck, should we start worrying?" I say.

Mark replies, "No, I'm sure Hoime is with him."

Mark joins us on the shore. Fifteen minutes later, here they come around the bend. Even from this distance, we can see Fralia is hammered, and Hoime isn't happy about it. We meet them at the shore and help drunken Fralia out of the raft. It's all he can do to stumble over to my tube and pass out.

Hoime then tells us, "Harris. Your buddy has a drinking problem. I saved his life back there. He fell out of his tube at the second rapids while trying to get a beer out of the cooler. He was bobbing downstream. Finally, he got caught in some wood debris, and I was able to pull him out of it. I've seen guys like him before. I'm telling you—he has a drinking problem."

I apologize, tell him thanks, and think, *We'll be home in a week, and he'll no longer be my problem.*

Hoime

It was a keen observation from Hoime. At that age, everyone drank to excess more than once. Some guys seemed to get more hammered than others, but the concept of a drinking problem or one of my friends having a problem never entered my mind.

"If you're up for it, we're going to cruise the Sunrise Mall. Eight o'clock," says Hoime.

"We'll see. It depends on how my drunk friend is doing. I'm not going to leave him at my aunt's house alone."

"Okay. Hopefully, we see you. We'll be in Jeff's '69 red Charger."

◆ ◆ ◆

Like he does, Fralia rallies, and we are off to do the next Sacramento thing: cruise the Sunrise Mall. We park poor, oil-leaking, out-of-place Herman in a parking lot away from the cruise and walk over. Being from San Diego, we thought we had cornered the market on hot chicks, but this spectacle is making us rethink that.

The sun is going down, and the action is heating up. Hundreds of people are driving back and forth with their windows rolled all the way down. Most of the girls are in tube tops, halter tops, or summer dresses, showing off their tans. They are hanging their heads out of the windows, the breeze blowing their long, beautiful hair as they smile, giggle, flirt, and blow kisses. The guys have their arms hanging out, pressing against the door, flexing their biceps and trying to look tough.

It's like *American Graffiti*, but this is 1978, not 1962. It's a two-way parade with lowriders, grease monkeys, college kids, and high schoolers—all vying for attention in their super-clean cars.

We spot Jeff in his '69 red Charger with Hoime riding shotgun. At the light, they wave us over, and we jump in the back seat. Hoime wastes no time and gets right on Fralia.

"How you feeling, buddy?"

"Great. I had a blast floating the American."

"Do you remember it?"

"Most of it. I do remember hanging onto a branch and you rescuing me. So thanks for that, but it's a blur."

"So you're feeling all right?"

"I'm ready to roll."

Hoime just shakes his head.

We are no longer spectators on the sidewalk—now we are part of the action, and the perspective is entirely different. All the cruisers may not be friends, but they recognize each other. This is our first cruising experience. We know they do it in Escondido, but if you live in Rancho Peñasquitos—or, as we call it, PQ—you don't go to Escondido unless you are going to the army surplus store or Farrell's Ice Cream Parlour.

Like at the river, the guys know just about everyone. Danny and Barb pass by in a convertible VW Bug and yell, "Greggy!"

"Whoa," says Fralia. "You know those chicks?"

"Yeah, dude. Of course, I know them. I spent more than two hours with them and two of their friends earlier today."

"Really?"

"Yes. You were getting fucked up and missed it all," I tell him.

"Damn, Danny is looking really good," says Hoime, shaking his head.

"Dude, she's hot. Jeff told me you two had a little thing going your sophomore year."

"We did, but I was dumb. Maybe I should pull her off the pile."

"Dude, I would," I tell him.

Jeff says, "Don't. She's hot, but she's not worth it."

It is quite a scene. There are rich girls from Christian Brothers High School cruising their parents' brand-new Mercedes-Benzes. We see a sweet, low-rider Impala and a few cars from the late '50s but mostly muscle cars from the late '60s and early '70s: GTOs, Firebirds, a Chevelle SS, Mustangs, an Olds 442, a Challenger, and even a Barracuda—and dozens of Camaros. The most bitchin' car—hands down—is a red 1970 Torino GT 429 Super Cobra Jet.

For a brief moment, we both flip out, thinking we see Jules when a yellow Opel GT identical to hers passes us. It really gets us thinking about home.

◆ ◆ ◆

We could stay in Sac longer, but we are both longing to get home, and we have one more stop in San Jose to see our friend Suzie. I call her when we wake up and tell her we'll be there for lunch. Kahl shows up as we are loading up so we only have a brief opportunity to talk and take a family photo. I hope things work out for him.

Myself, Kahl, Aunt Dot, and Ty

SAN JOSE

Suzie is our confidante and dear friend. It was a bummer when she moved to San Jose our junior year, but we have kept in touch.

Before Suzie moved, her house was the hangout place. And lucky me, she lived just down the street. She had a pool and a Jacuzzi. And her mom, Nancy—or, as we called her, Nance—was the coolest. Everything started innocently enough our sophomore year. Then we all started getting our driver's licenses. Then came the drinking and smoking pot. By the time Suzie was getting ready to move, the age of innocence was over, and all the dynamics changed.

There were breakups, blowups, friendships tested, and hormones running amok. Guys were full of bravado and acting tough, trying to impress the girls. Suzie was invaluable to us, always willing to share the female perspective and straight out tell us when we were dicks, which was often. Fools suffered greatly in her presence. As strong as the hold Suzie had over us was, things sometimes still got out of control. The classic story, of course, had Fralia at the center of it.

While partying at Suzie's one night, half of us were drinking; the other half, myself included, really weren't into drinking yet. Fralia was in the Jacuzzi entertaining three girls with his stories. Kenny, one of our classmates, found an empty Jack Daniel's bottle, filled it halfway with his piss, and told all of us in the kitchen to watch through the window. He went outside and slowly walked past the Jacuzzi with the Jack Daniel's bottle.

Fralia said, "Kenny, give me that bottle."

We didn't need to hear the conversation; it was easy to surmise what was happening by their gestures and reading their lips.

Kenny was playing Fralia like a fiddle.

"No, you don't want this, Fralia."

"Yes, I do, Goddammit. Give me that bottle."

"No."

"Dammit!"

"Fralia, no. It's not for you."

"Don't make me get out of this Jacuzzi."

The three girls wistfully watched Fralia, thinking he was cool.

Kenny said, "Okay, here."

Fralia, as Fralia does, made a big show out of grabbing the bottle, holding it up, unscrewing the cap, and tilting his head back. All the while, we were watching the show through the kitchen window.

At the same time the bottle touched his lips, we all started to yell, "Don't!" even though he couldn't hear us.

But it was too late. He took a big swig of piss and spit it out in a mist, spraying his fawning fan club. We all ran out back to break up the fight before it had a chance to happen.

◆ ◆ ◆

The first thing out of Suzie's mouth when we arrive in San Jose is, "Drink any piss lately, Fralia?"

"Fuck off, Suzie."

Friendship is a beautiful thing.

Nance is at the store buying food and beers for us. While we wait, the three of us sit around the pool and shoot the shit. Suzie tells us her friend, Kim, is coming over.

"Really? Is she hot?" Fralia asks.

"Not in the obvious way you two always fall for," replies Suzie.

"What in the hell does that mean?" I say, slightly offended.

"Come on. You boys are all the same. It's always the beautiful blond SoCal girl who turns your heads."

"Like AJ!" blurts out Fralia.

"Who?" asks Suzie.

"A beautiful blond we met in Idaho who turned our heads, and Fralia is still dreaming about," I say.

"See? So predictable," Suzie says, shaking her head.

"So what's Kim's deal?" Fralia wants to know.

"Well, she's my friend."

"Then that's good enough for us," we both say.

"She was raised Mormon, but she gave that up a long time ago." And then Suzie whispers, "Truthfully, I think she might be a nympho."

"What?" we both say, all bug-eyed.

"I already told her, under no circumstance will she be doing both or either of you."

"What? A nympho?" we both say, still bug-eyed.

"I never should have told you. Just be cool when she gets here."

Fralia says, "It's going to be hard to unhear that."

"Well, do your best," Suzie says.

"Where's your little brother?" I ask.

"Who knows where Tony is? Probably smoking pot somewhere with his loser friends."

Nance opens the sliding glass door, smiles and says, "Hi guys! How about a little help bringing in the groceries?"

It's so awesome to see her. We both jump up and give her a big hug. Then bring in the groceries.

Nance and Fralia

Listening to Suzie and Nance, we sense Suzie had a hard time settling into San Jose. It was tough to go to a new school during her junior year. Her popularity wasn't the same, and it weighed on her. We could tell she really missed us by all the good-natured ribbing she was dishing out, mostly directed at Fralia.

We hadn't even had a beer yet, and somehow, while skimming the debris out of the pool, Fralia fell in fully clothed. Suzie, Nance, and I laugh our asses off. That's when Kim walks through the gate. And she also laughs.

The rest of the evening, us four high-school grads lounge around the pool, sip beers, jump in and out of the water, and give Fralia a hard time.

Kim is all right—nothing like what we were expecting. She is kind of a plain Jane, but she comes off as being super smart, and she isn't even flirty. If we weren't told she might be a nympho, we would have never guessed it. Then again, neither of us has ever met one. But Fralia swears there's such a thing. He claims it's a mental disorder, and eventually they go completely nuts and end up in the funny farm.

Suzie's friend, Ann, calls to tell her she scored us free passes for Six Flags, where she works, and that she would leave them at the front gate tomorrow. Just show up any time after noon.

In our room, before falling asleep, the realization that the trip is ending hits us.

"Six Flags tomorrow and then the next day, southbound," Fralia says.

"And back to living with our parents!" I respond.

"Geez, how depressing."

"And getting jobs and going to Palomar Junior College,"
I say.

"Geez, how depressing," Fralia repeats.

"Get over it. Let's have a blast tomorrow," I say.

"Oh, don't worry about that!"

◆ ◆ ◆

Herman got a much-deserved day off while Suzie drove her
Bug to Six Flags.

"Shotgun!" Fralia yells, jumping into the front seat.

"Go ahead. It'll be nice to have the whole backseat to myself," I say.

A few miles later:

"Fuck. Turn off that Fleetwood Mac shit. I can't stand
Rumors," I whine.

"What do you want to hear?" Suzie says, annoyed.

"*Fly Like an Eagle*," spews the Steve Miller wannabe.

I just shake my head and say, "Geez. Both of you are killing me...Fleetwood Mac and Steve Miller. God help me."

"You two are worse than girls. Just sit there like Ken
dolls and shut the fuck up! For old times' sake, I'm putting in
Madman across the Water."

We both shut up, but only for a few minutes.

"Your brother gave me a doobie this morning for us to
smoke before entering Six Flags," Fralia says and grins.

"Tony gave you a doobie? I worry about him. My mom
caught him pouring vodka in his Cheerios for breakfast. I
think he's going to break her heart," Suzie says.

"I hope not," is the only thing I could think of to say.

"Are we going to see this Ann chick?" Fralia wants to know.

"I know where she usually works. I'm sure we can track her down."

"Free passes are pretty sweet. She's got to be a cool chick," I comment.

"If you're going to spark that doob, do it now while we're driving. The parking lot has security crawling all over it," Suzie tells Fralia.

"Are you partaking? I know Harris isn't."

"Yeah. I'll have a hit," says Suzie.

"You know, 'Tiny Dancer' is the first song I slow danced to," I comment as the song begins.

"No shit," they both say. "With Heather."

"We've both heard you say that a million times," Fralia says.

"You sure can be sentimental, can't you?" Suzie says.

"He's a sap," Fralia says while choking on smoke.

I snap back at him, "Have another hit, Fralia."

"Don't mind if I do!"

Suzie parks her Bug. It's one o'clock, and the parking lot is packed. We jump on a shuttle wagon that takes us right to the window where our passes are waiting. We feel like VIPs.

"I need some cotton candy," Fralia says.

"Geez. You already have the munchies!" Suzie exclaims.

"Shit. I haven't smoked any pot all summer. There's no way I was going to be carrying in some of the states we visited. They'd lock you up and throw away the key for a little dime bag. That and Harris wouldn't let me."

Fralia gets his cotton candy and commences to get the sticky, sugary stuff all over his face and hair. Suzie and I laugh hysterically. He's such an easy target for Suzie, and she shows him no mercy. But it's all in fun.

We hit all the rides and scream our heads off. Fralia gets nauseous, but he recovers without vomiting. That was disappointing. We were both hoping he would blow chunks. We meet Ann and thank her for the free passes.

She says, "Anything for Suzie's friends. Even you two guys!" Then she laughs.

Suzie invites Ann over for pizza that night. "I can't wait. I'm off at seven, and I'll head straight over."

We get back to Suzie's house, and she tells Nance the plan. Nance is agreeable and says she'll even buy beer for us if we all promise to stay there—even Ann. We all promise. Why would we want to go anywhere else? Pizza, beer, Jacuzzi, music—we are all set!

Ann is a real firecracker. She and Suzie have us laughing so hard that we cry and our jaws hurt. The stories they tell are unbelievable, but they swear they are all true.

Tony makes a brief appearance and then disappears with Fralia.

Suzie just shakes her head and says, "That's my brother."

Moments later, Fralia reappears, all smiles.

"Suzie, will Nance mind if we smoke a little pot?"

"For you, she'd probably make an exception, especially since we promised not to go anywhere."

"Girls, you want a little puff? Gregory can just watch."

Fralia hits it hard, but the girls not so much.

He announces, "This is our last night, so I'm going big. Go get us some more Coors, Harris."

"Four?" I question the group.

"Five," chirps Fralia. "And find a church key. I'm going to shotgun one."

"Oh, boy. Look out! Fralia is on a roll," I say.

After he shotguns a beer, he belches and barks, "Suzie, do you still have the *Eagles Greatest Hits* album?"

"Yes."

"Well, put it on! Somehow, we didn't bring any Eagles on the trip. And it reminds me of the good old days when you lived in PQ. I have great memories of those times, except, of course, the piss night."

"I was just getting ready to tell Ann that story!" Suzie says and smiles.

"Please don't," begs Fralia.

"Okay. I'll wait until you two leave." Suzie laughs.

"What's everyone's favorite song on the album?" I ask.

"'Take it Easy,' hands down," says Fralia. "I mean, come on! What great lyrics!"

"Ha! Of course, that's your song, Fralia. 'Lyin' Eyes' is the song, period," admonishes Suzie.

"'Desperado,'" I say.

Fralia quickly responds with, "I told you he was a sap."

"You're all saps," says Ann. "Eagles. Give me a break. It must be the SoCal in you three."

"Blasphemy," retorts Fralia.

"If you want to hear some real music, listen to Patti Smith," claims Ann.

"Who?" Fralia says.

"That's what I thought," Ann says. "Get your hands on her new release, *Easter*, and listen to 'Because the Night' over and over. That's passion. Suzie and Greg will get it, but I have my doubts that you will."

Suzie smiles, shakes her head, and says in the way only she can, "Fuckin' Fralia."

After a few more runs to the refrigerator, the night becomes a blur.

In the morning, we are both groggy. Ann and Suzie are still asleep. We head directly to the kitchen, looking for nourishment.

"Good morning, boys," Nance cheerily greets us.

"Did we embarrass ourselves last night?" Fralia asks.

Nance smiles. "Only a little. The girls certainly got a kick out of you two."

"We got a kick out of them too," I respond.

"How are your heads?" Nance inquires.

"A little food and we'll be better than great," proclaims Fralia.

"Well, I made you two a little care package for your drive home. Let me wake up the girls, and I'll cook us all breakfast."

"Thanks, Nance. You're the best," Fralia says.

Nance just smiles.

The girls appear to be in the same shape as us. Breakfast gives us life, and we start recapping the evening. And laugh all over again.

For some reason, I'm really itching to get home, so I finally announce, "It's time for us to hit the road."

We all hug and say our farewells. Driving away, I see all three of them in the rearview mirror, standing in the street, waving goodbye. It makes me a little sad.

Ann and Suzie

SOUTHBOUND, PUT THE HAMMER DOWN

"Let's fill Herman up with gas and oil, and head straight home," I say.

"You don't want to cruise down the 101?" Fralia says, grinning.

"Fuck, no! We're done. Straight down I-5, across that shitty 78, through your favorite shithole town, Escondido, and then drop you off at your house."

"You're so predictable, Harris."

"It's time to go home."

"You're right. It is," he agrees.

"How much money do we have left?" I ask.

"Sixty bucks. We'll need one more tank of gas after this one. No need to buy food since Nance hooked us up with sandwiches and snacks. We'll put our oil collector under Herman at every stop. So we'll probably both have at least twenty dollars in our pockets when we hit San Diego. And we might as well shoot all the film we have in our cameras."

"Might as well. I hope we got some good pictures, but they'll probably all be overexposed," I say, being a Negative Ned.

"Yours might be with that shitty old camera your dad let you use. Mine are going to be great. Get slides, and we'll have a big slideshow party."

There really isn't any conversation as we drive through Central Valley. We are both in deep thought, pondering the trip and our unknown future. We don't play any tapes—not even Fralia's favorite, *Fly Like an Eagle*.

South of Bakersfield, before the Grapevine, we start scanning the radio for LA stations. We aren't impressed with the music. In one hour, we hear "Band on the Run" four times. Give me a break! That is so 1974. So we have fun and start bashing everything we hate about Los Angeles, especially the Dodgers.

Once we clear Camp Pendleton and hit the 78, we both get quiet again. I'm unexpectedly overcome with a flood of emotions. The sensation is a little unnerving. I clear my throat to break up the solitude.

Sometimes when I'm uncomfortable, I just can't keep myself from being a dick. "Are you bracing yourself for the drive through Escondido?" I laugh.

"You know I hate that shithole city."

Still laughing, I say, "Oh, I know. I just don't know why."

"I can't explain it, Harris, but I do."

"You know, five weeks is a long time to spend with one person," I state the obvious.

"Ha! You're not kidding!"

"Well, we actually did it," I say.

"I never had a doubt," Fralia replies. "And I'll tell you what, Harris. If you ask me, we learned more on this trip than we did in four years of high school."

"Look at you. Getting all philosophical."

"It's true," he says.

"All I know is we have stories to last a lifetime," I tell him.

"Like AJ, psycho Robert, West Yellowstone bar hopping, and I'll never forget that bald eagle," he replies.

"And you almost drowning in the American River!" I say.

"Yeah, I really owe your guy Hoime," Fralia says sincerely.

"You do. Thank God, you didn't die," I tell him.

"Gregory, nothing is going to take me out," Fralia resolutely states.

"Invincible, huh?"

"You know it!"

"What are you going to do when we get home?" I ask.

"Don't take it personally, but I'm *not* going to see you!"

"Trust me, Fralia, the feeling is mutual. Like I said, five weeks with one person is a long time. I'm sick of you!"

"Yeah. The VW and the two-man tent got smaller every week. It's a good thing we're friends," he says.

"If we didn't kill each other after five weeks, I'm sure we'll be friends forever. But right now, I'm done looking at your greasy, matted hair and smelling your B.O."

"Ha! Next time you hear 'Fly Like an Eagle,' you'll think of me, and I guarantee you'll smile."

TUESDAY, MAY 4, 1993

Once the mid '80s rolled around, Fralia and I kind of drifted apart. We were still friends, but we just didn't see each other often. When we did, without fail, the summer of '78 would come up. We both remembered it in detail. It was a magical period in our lives. The further removed from that summer, the more we appreciated it. Life and living were easy then.

My recollections of 1991 to 1993 are vague at best. Sometime during late 1991, or maybe even early 1992, I got a phone call from Fralia. He was living in his favorite city, Escondido, with Laura, his second wife, and his young son, Christopher. Laura had kicked him out, and he needed a temporary place to stay. I was living by myself in a two-bedroom condo in Rancho Bernardo, so, of course, I told him he was welcome to stay at my place. After all, that's what friends are for.

I honestly can't remember how long we were roommates, but it was for sure over a year. The restaurant company two friends and I started, Fins A Mexican Eatery, was over three years old, and we had recently opened our second location. I was working over seventy hours a week, and any free time was spent with my girlfriend, Cecile. Fralia was a general manager at Hungry Hunter and also working a lot, so even though we were living together, we really didn't hang out much. The carefree days of our youth were over. We were both doing our best to grind our way through adulthood, but it was evident he wasn't doing well.

The twinkle in his eye was gone. My friend was spiraling downward. His second failed marriage emotionally wrecked him. His drinking accelerated. It quickly began to impact his job performance and his life. He was once great at his job, a real rising star and the youngest general manager in the entire Hungry Hunter chain. His company became so concerned, they paid for him to go to a rehab program. When he came out of rehab, he was on Antabuse to prevent him from drinking. It worked for a while, and occasionally, I would catch a glimpse of the 1978 version of Dave Fralia, but it was short-lived. He got off the Antabuse and started drinking again—hard.

One evening while he was at work at the Hungry Hunter in Imperial Beach, he called me and sounded really lonely. He wanted to know if I would come down for dinner. It would be his treat. So I did. When I arrived I could tell he wasn't drunk, but he was mentally in a bad place and saying strange things. I knew I had to get him out of there before he said or did something really stupid in front of a guest or one of his employees. I convinced him to leave early. He agreed but only if I would follow him to a bar. The next thing I knew, we were parking our cars at a titty bar in Kearny Mesa. Apparently, he was spending a lot of time there, and every girl knew his name.

His bosses were very disappointed he had relapsed, and they fired him. Losing his job was a punishing blow to his self-esteem, and his drinking got even worse. He had a hard time finding work, and once he found some, he couldn't hold on to the job. He tried to pick up a few shifts waiting tables at different restaurants, but that didn't really work out. At one point, he was working for a flower distributor and would bring home roses every day, but that job required him to wake up at four in the morning and be at work by five. Every morning, his loud alarm would go off and wake Cecile and me up, but not him. Needless to say, that job also didn't last long.

As I mentioned, my recollections of this time period are vague at best. However, Tuesday, May 4, 1993, is a day I'll never forget. Late afternoon that day, Fralia came home hammered and crashed into my neighbor's brand-new Nissan Maxima while swinging into a parking spot. Everyone could hear the collision. My neighbor and I came out to see what was going on. Fralia was still behind the wheel of his Nissan pickup with a blank stare on his face. Sue, my neighbor, was irate that he'd crashed into her parked car. I got Fralia out of his truck. There were empty vodka bottles scattered around the cab. I asked Sue to let me get him upstairs, and we would handle the insurance stuff later. She trusted me and agreed.

Cecile and I were practically living together at my place, but she still had her own apartment, and that evening I had plans to go to her place for dinner. Before leaving, I read Fralia the Riot Act. I really laid into him and told him he needed to get his shit together. And since he was so fucked up, under no circumstance was he to leave the condo. I'd be back in a couple of hours.

Over dinner, Cecile and I talked about the latest Fralia incident. I told her it was really bad this time. Talking with her, I became concerned about the guns in the house. We both agreed we needed to get back there and check on him.

When we got back to the condo, Fralia's dad, Tom, and his brother, Ron, were there, but Fralia wasn't, and his truck was still in the parking lot. Tom told us he'd gotten a call from Laura. Fralia had called her and wanted to talk to his son to tell him he loved him. Laura could overhear the conversation and was afraid it was a final goodbye.

I checked the guns, and one was missing. On his bed, we found a rambling cryptic letter about being a failure. We called the police, but because he was an adult, they needed to wait longer before filing a missing person's report.

We started calling friends, hoping someone came over and picked him up. We also checked the local bars I knew he frequented. We were frantic. The next day seemed to last forever. The condo became a home base for his family and friends. We scoured the open space behind the neighborhood and went to the liquor store where he always bought his vodka. The clerk had seen him yesterday during the day, but not since then. As the day dragged on, we felt like we had been through an emotional wringer. We couldn't shake the sense of despair that was overcoming us. *What if we never know what happened? What if we never find him? What if...*

That evening, Cecile went to go get us all dinner. As she was driving out of the condo complex, she looked across the street and up the hill. You could call it intuition, but she knew Fralia was up there. When she came back with dinner, she told me about her suspicion, but I shot it down and told her we had already looked up there.

The next day, May 6, Cecile and I tried going to work. The Fralia family was still at the condo, hoping for the best. Cecile's bad feeling just wouldn't go away, so on her lunch break, she came over to the condo to change her shoes so she could hike up the hill. Fralia's sister, Connie, was lying on his bed staring at the ceiling and crying. Not fully realizing what was about to take place, Cecile suggested that Connie get out of the condo for a little bit and come with her.

Unknown to them, they were tracing his final steps, through the parking lot, across the street, and then up the concrete culvert on the hill. Connie led the way and was the first to see her brother's body. She screamed hysterically. Then Cecile saw him, and she started screaming. Neither of them could stop. A neighbor from the closest house ran outside and called 911. The police showed up. A helicopter was flying above the location of his body. Someone called me at work with the news. I don't remember arriving on the scene or anything that happened afterward. It's a complete blur.

He killed himself on Tuesday, May 4, 1993, with the .22 caliber rifle he had on our summer of '78 trip. A single shot to the heart.

That tragic day will forever haunt us.

ACKNOWLEDGMENTS

This book could not have been written without with the encouragement and help from the following folks.

First and foremost, my wonderful wife, Amy, who translated my scribbling into a Word document and tried in vain to teach me about commas. Thanks for reading the manuscript over and over again. I definitely tested your patience, but you continued to encourage me.

Jean Chalupsky for always having a quick answer to my numerous grammatical questions. English teachers are awesome!

Dave House and Nick Garbarini for the beers, early reads, and reminiscing with me about Fralia.

Andrea Nissley, Bill Nolte, Thomas Eidam, and R. Gary Perkins for the early reads, storyline help, and editing.

Jenny Chandler at Elite Authors for her guidance throughout the entire self-publishing process.

Cecile Hinton for providing clarity to May 4-6, 1993 and for being there.

Christine Dianni for the beautiful hand drawn map of the route, helping with the cover design decision, and catching mistakes.

And last but not least, my Uncle Butch for encouraging me to write a book. I wish he were alive to read it.

Greg Harris is a fifth-generation Californian who's lived in San Diego since 1974. A former restaurateur and currently a semi-retired consultant, Greg loves nothing more than to ride his single speed mountain bike and travel in his twenty-five-foot Airstream with his wife, Amy, a kindergarten teacher. You can read about their adventures on <u>anotherboldmove.com</u>.

51919143R00069

Made in the USA
San Bernardino, CA
04 September 2019